Effective Study and Learning
How to Help

Gavin Reid and Jennie Guise

Effective Study and Learning

© Pavilion Publishing & Media

The authors have asserted their rights in accordance with the Copyright, Designs and Patents Act (1988) to be identified as the authors of this work.

Published by:
Pavilion Publishing and Media Ltd
Blue Sky Offices, 25 Cecil Pashley Way
Shoreham-by-Sea, West Sussex
BN43 5FF

Tel: 01273 434 943
Email: info@pavpub.com
Web: www.pavpub.com

Published 2021

All rights reserved. No part of this publication may be reproduced, stored in a retrieval system, or transmitted in any form or by any means, electronic, mechanical, photocopying, recording or otherwise, without prior permission in writing of the publisher and the copyright owners.

A catalogue record for this book is available from the British Library.

ISBN: 978-1-912755-90-5

Pavilion Publishing and Media is a leading publisher of books, training materials and digital content in mental health, social care and allied fields. Pavilion and its imprints offer must-have knowledge and innovative learning solutions underpinned by sound research and professional values.

Authors: Gavin Reid and Jennie Guise
Cover design: Emma Dawe, Pavilion Publishing and Media Ltd
Page layout and typesetting: Phil Morash, Pavilion Publishing and Media Ltd
Printing: CMP

Contents

Series Preface v
About the Authors vi
Authors' Preface vii
How to Use This Book ix

Part 1: Introduction 1
    Chapter 1: What is learning? 3
    Chapter 2: Readiness to learn 7
    Chapter 3: The learning environment 11
    Chapter 4: The process of learning 17
    Ten key things to know about study and learning 22

Part 2: Personal and interpersonal issues 23
    Chapter 5: Self-efficacy and self-esteem 25
    Chapter 6: Motivation 31
    Chapter 7: Stress and anxiety 39

Part 3: The learning environment 43
    Chapter 8: Barriers to learning 45
    Chapter 9: The school ethos 49
    Chapter 10: Feedback 53
    Chapter 11: Metacognition – understanding how you learn 55
    Chapter 12: Classroom design 63
    Chapter 13: Differentiation 69

Part 4: The learning process 79
    Chapter 14: Time management and organisation 83
    Chapter 15: Information-gathering 87
    Chapter 16: Note-taking 93
    Chapter 17: Linking new information to prior knowledge 101
    Chapter 18: Problem-solving skills 109
    Chapter 19: Understanding what is being taught 113

Chapter 20: Making subject teaching learner-friendly 121
Chapter 21: Supporting and improving memory 131
Chapter 22: Active information processing 141

Part 5: Essay-writing, exams and lifelong learning 147

Chapter 23: Planning and writing a good essay 149
Chapter 24: Effective revision 155
Chapter 25: Exam preparation 163
Chapter 26: Sitting the exam 169
Chapter 27: Lifelong learning 179

Part 6: Conclusion 189

Chapter 28: Summary 191
Chapter 29: A last word to parents and carers 199
Chapter 30: A last word to teachers and schools 201

Index of *How to Help* advice 203
Appendices 205
References 215

Series Preface

Young people in today's society face considerable stresses. The Prince's Trust, which has monitored youth opinion for ten years, found that just under half of young people who use social media now feel more anxious about their future when they compare themselves to others on websites and apps such as Instagram, Twitter and Facebook. A similar proportion agreed that social media makes them feel 'inadequate'. The *Guardian Weekly* noted in early 2019 that more than half of young people think that social media creates 'overwhelming pressure' to succeed.

There are many issues that are likely to affect every pupil at some point during his or her time at school. How these are dealt with can be 'make or break' for some pupils, because of the crucial stages in education that can be affected. The implications are deep and broad because, understandably, the child's experience of education, and his or her success at school, can have a tremendous impact on later life chances.

The *How to Help* series covers a broad and comprehensive range of topics that will have resonance for today's parents, carers and educators. Each title is designed to make a valuable contribution in the breadth of issues that it introduces, and the realistic helping strategies that it puts forward.

Gavin Reid and Jennie Guise
Series Editors

About the Authors

Gavin Reid is an international Practitioner Psychologist, consultant and author. He was a classroom teacher and university lecturer and has written more than thirty-five books in the field of dyslexia and learning. His books have been translated into seven languages. He currently lectures worldwide, and he has regular international consultancies. He is Chair of the British Dyslexia Association Accreditation Board. He has sat on government panels on assessment, and he has been engaged in several United Nations-funded projects as a learning difficulties expert on assessment and learning.

Jennie Guise is a Practitioner Psychologist and author. She has worked in research, and now in applied practice as founder and Director of Dysguise Ltd. Her main interests are in identifying what will help individual learners to progress and in helping to break down, or work around, the many and various barriers that can affect learning. She works collaboratively with educators to apply that knowledge in practical ways.

Authors' Preface

Welcome to this book on learning and studying. It is part of the 'How to Help' series, and we aim to focus on exactly that perspective. We intend to speak to a wide readership, so the book is geared to primary, secondary and tertiary education sectors and we also envisage that some students in further and higher education may benefit from it. We hope that teachers, parents and learners themselves will all be able to use it in a variety of ways as a learning and teaching tool.

The book is designed as a toolkit for learning, and therefore as well as looking at practical strategies we also explore the underlying principles of learning. We have both had many years of experience of teaching children, young people and adults, and in carrying out assessments for learners who are experiencing difficulties. These involve an analysis of the learner's strengths and areas of weakness, with a view to providing strategies that will help that person to achieve his or her learning potential. We have also had countless conversations with pupils, parents, carers and teachers about the kinds of things that can have an impact on taking in information, understanding it, retaining it and demonstrating their knowledge through various types of assessment. We have drawn on this experience and on a wide range of research in the areas of learning and studying in writing this book.

A key part of our day-to-day work is to provide accessible and helpful information to pupils, parents, carers and schools about how best to support individual learners. We firmly believe in the importance of all parties working together towards the same aim, and in being supported to do so, and this is an underpinning principle of this book. In each chapter, we provide some background information and research and follow it with practical ways of helping in that particular area. We begin by looking at issues relating to the pupil's mindset – confidence, motivation and anxiety. We then move to the learning environment of the school and home. It is important for learners and those working with them to have a good understanding of the learning process, and this is discussed before moving on to the more specific areas of essay-writing and exam preparation.

We have aimed to make the book as comprehensive as possible, and on that basis we have incorporated ideas and strategies for all ages in relation to memory, learning and studying.

Having come through the school and university systems ourselves, we are well aware of the hurdles and challenges faced by students, and we have kept this in mind at all times while writing this book. This has also motivated us to include a chapter on lifelong learning. The foundations for this are often formed at school, but the skills involved in effective learning are utilised throughout life, irrespective of one's education or career.

We hope you find this book useful, and that it will assist you in your work and your interactions with children and young people. Above all, we hope that it will help you to assist them in the development of learning skills, and to empower them to become self-sufficient and successful learners.

Gavin Reid
Jennie Guise

How to Use This Book

Topics in this *How to Help* book are organised within four major sections, comprising Parts 2 to 5:

- Personal and interpersonal issues
- The learning environment
- The learning process
- Essay-writing, exams and lifelong learning

Within these sections, each topic is discussed in a separate chapter (although it should be noted that in practice there will frequently be areas of overlap), with advice for parents, carers teachers and schools. You can read through the sections in order or go straight to what most concerns you most. The topics have been chosen to represent the key issues that typically impact abilities in studying and learning, and which therefore require identification, adaptation and support.

 Whenever you see the *How to Help* icon, you can expect to find practical, ready to use suggestions and strategies for helping children and young people to build and maintain their levels of wellbeing and resilience.

We recommend that you read in full the Introduction (Part 1) and the Conclusion (Part 6). The former serves as an entry point into the main chapters, presenting the subject and core principles relating to it along with a list of ten essential things to know. The latter summarises the most important points for readers to take away, and offers final comments for parents, carers, teachers and schools.

To keep up to date with the *How to Help* series, bookmark:
www.pavpub.com/howtohelp

> "Learning how to learn is life's most important skill."
>
> Tony Buzan

Part 1: Introduction

Chapter 1: What is learning?

Introducing study and learning

Study and learning skills are fundamental to successful outcomes in education, and eventually in the workplace. Many students exert considerable effort in 'studying' but still come away disappointed with the outcomes, particularly when faced with traditional, written exams. All too often, they fall short of fulfilling their potential not because of a lack of hard work, but simply because they are not skilled enough in learning. They have failed to grasp sufficiently that the core characteristics of successful learning are self-knowledge and, alongside it, knowledge on how to learn as effectively as possible.

As authors and practitioner psychologists, we fully embrace the sentiments of Professor John Hattie when he suggests that "the kids who knuckle down and get the right answers do not always succeed... we have oodles of tests on achievement, but I want to measure learning" (*Weekend Australian*, 18 July 2014).[1] This suggests that education should focus more on learning and, in particular, how learners can progress from surface learning to deep learning. 'Learning to learn' is therefore a fundamental cornerstone of this book. Rather than children accepting our learning strategies, we aim to equip them to develop their own. Certainly we offer a wealth of guidance, but we also promote independence – an essential ingredient for positive self-esteem and intrinsic motivation.

> ### Expert View
> *"The kids who knuckle down and get the right answers do not always succeed... we have oodles of tests on achievement, but I want to measure learning."*
>
> John Hattie

This book focuses on strategies for effective study and learning, and also looks at the underlying skills required for effective learning and successful study. These include personal strategies that the learner must develop for him- or herself. We explore why knowledge of one's own learning style and preferences is important, including the most effective environment for learning, and we explore the role of the school in equipping learners for study. We also discuss the management of learning and the choices learners have to make in relation to managing their

---

[1] Hattie J (2014) The Kids Who Knuckle Down And Get The Right Answers Do Not Always Succeed. *Weekend Australian*, July 2018.

study, whether it be homework or preparing for exams. Finally, there is an increasing number of applications and resources designed to help learners of all ages with study. Some of these are evaluated, and some of our own are included.

At school we learn languages, science formulas, about the environment and nature, literature and a host of other topics – but learning how to learn is not always seen as a priority. Often it is an add-on and sometimes a timetable filler, which can have the undesired effect of students equating studying with memory! Writing notes from a text is neither study nor learning, but simply a writing exercise. We feel strongly that study and learning skills should be included in the curriculum for all children, including those in the early strategies of education, and that by learning to study more efficiently and effectively, children and young people can gain the rewards justified by their endeavours.

> **Key Point**
>
> It is very important that students gain an understanding of how they learn, along with an appreciation of how to use that knowledge to improve their learning outcomes.

Let us begin with some key points to know about learning:

Learning is holistic
It is vital, as a starting point, to take account of the emotional and social needs of learners. Beyond this, environmental factors can be very important, and these should be considered in learning programmes for learners of all ages.

Learning is a process
It is important to consider this, as it implies that learning will take place in a series of steps and, importantly, these steps may have to be worked through in sequence. For example, it is difficult to memorise information if it is not fully understood.

Learning is more effective when the content is familiar
This is crucial, because students will only remember information well if they have understood it in the first place, and the best way of doing this is to locate it in the context of what they already know.

Learning styles differ

People have different skills, and this must be accounted for. For instance, they need sufficient time to complete tasks – while some learners acquire information quickly, others may need more time. It is very important that students gain an understanding of how they learn, along with an appreciation of how to use that knowledge to improve their learning outcomes. They will also benefit from different approaches to teaching, and different ways of assessing what they have learned.

Education systems and the wider context

Modern learning theory recognises the contribution of experience, reflection, social interaction and practice in the development of ideas and skills, and it acknowledges the importance of developmental stages. Teachers also recognise that how best to teach depends very much on what is being taught. While debates about best practices still go on, driven partly by disagreements about the purpose of education, there is broad consensus regarding how people learn – and how best they can study.

> *Key Point*
>
> *By learning to study effectively, students can develop some important skills and come to know themselves better as individuals and learners.*

Today, while academic knowledge clearly still has a critical role to play in education, we use the Internet to discover facts and recruiters seek graduates who have not only passed academic exams but are also skilled in creativity, collaboration, critical thinking, and problem-solving. By learning to study effectively, students can develop some of these important skills and come to know themselves better as individuals and learners, at the same time as acquiring academic knowledge and storing it more effectively as a result.

Chapter 2: Readiness to learn

A holistic approach

There are many challenges faced by learners in today's education system. Some of them relate directly to learning, but others are personal, interpersonal and environmental issues that can prevent the student from functioning effectively in the learning situation. Learning therefore needs to be viewed from a whole-person perspective, and a holistic approach to its planning is necessary.

> **Key Point**
>
> *The capacity of the human brain to store information is unlimited, yet the most significant factor in learning is often failure to recall.*

In this and the following two chapters, we will put the most important issues into context and highlight the key challenges for parents, carers and professionals, as well as learners themselves, when advocating and developing effective learning strategies. These challenges will be developed more fully throughout the book. While there is inevitably overlap between areas, even more so in the real world, for the sake of clarity we will look in turn at personal and interpersonal challenges, challenges related to the learning environment, challenges related to the process of study and learning, and finally challenges related specifically to essay-writing, exams and lifelong learning.

The right frame of mind

We often hear children and adults of all ages indicate that they are not bright – often in derogatory and self-deprecating language. This 'inbuilt' expectation of academic failure can be immensely destructive for the learning process. One of the key tasks for educators, therefore, is to try to reverse this attitude, and to instil in students a degree of self-confidence in their abilities.

The capacity of the human brain to store information is unlimited, yet the most significant factor in learning is often failure to recall. Recalling information is really all about making connections, which means learning effectively at the outset. It is important to get this message across to learners, and to stress that everyone is perfectly capable of learning well. Recall can be greatly affected by mood and outlook. It's like changing the wheel on a car – if you doubt your own abilities then it's likely to be a stressful experience with a potentially negative outcome, but once you have the tools, techniques and experience you can approach it fearlessly and be successful.

It is therefore a good investment of time to begin by paying attention to personal and interpersonal issues that can affect children and young people. By maximising controllable positive factors and minimising negative ones, we can ensure that learners are in the best possible frame of mind for learning.

Self-efficacy and self-esteem

The Canadian-American psychologist Albert Bandura (1977) introduced the notion of 'self-efficacy', which is somewhat similar to self-confidence in that it describes a person's expectation that he or she can achieve a certain type of behaviour.[2] In difficult situations, a person's beliefs about their own level of self-efficacy will affect how much stress he or she feels, along with their inclination to attempt the task in the first place. A general belief that you are capable of managing and succeeding may be viewed as a kind of preventative measure against stress, or at least a way to reduce the worst of its effects.

Expert View

"Self-efficacy refers to belief in one's agentive capabilities, that one can produce given levels of attainment."

Albert Bandura

Bandura's work was seminal, and its implications for how we deal with stress and life's challenges remain valid today. The most critical aspect of self-efficacy in relation to study and learning is that it has been shown that a person's level of self-efficacy can be improved. Given that self-efficacy directly influences results by affecting levels of stress and self-belief, it follows that an improvement in self-efficacy can lead to potential improvements in study and learning outcomes.

The most obvious way to improve self-efficacy is for an individual to have some experience of success. Once a successful experience is 'banked' in the memory, it can be drawn upon in times of difficulty to make the person feel more comfortable and capable. This can be critical for children and young people as they advance through school, and particularly when approaching higher education. Indeed, self-efficacy is an influential factor

---

2   Bandura A (1977) *Social Learning Theory*. Englewood Cliffs, NJ: Prentice Hall.

in academic achievement for learners of any age, especially in relation to their overall desire and enthusiasm to learn and succeed.

Another important aspect of self-efficacy theory is that it is crucial to take small steps that seem achievable, rather than to present learners with large or unstructured tasks that seem overwhelming and demoralising. Small steps are much more likely to lead to success, and success boosts self-efficacy. This creates a 'virtuous circle' that will help learners to keep moving in a positive direction.

Maintaining motivation

Motivation is a crucial component of learning, and ideally it should be intrinsic – that is, it should come from within the person. This means that the learner must want to achieve success for his or her own reasons – not because of some external (extrinsic) factor such as a reward, but because he or she sees some personal value and benefit in successfully completing the task.

As we have noted, motivation can be associated with self-efficacy and self-confidence – and self-confidence is a crucial factor in successful learning. Learners who lack self-confidence are unlikely to feel able to take responsibility for their own learning, or to develop a risk-taking approach to study and education. As a result they may lack the confidence to reveal their full knowledge of a topic in an exam for fear of being wrong, or because they simply don't believe that they could be right.

Key Point

Learners who lack self-confidence are unlikely to take responsibility for their own learning, or to develop a risk-taking approach to study and education.

In order to develop self-confidence, as we have seen, learners must have a perception of success – they must believe that they are capable of mastering the task and being successful. Some of this can relate to responsibility. If learners have the confidence to take control of their own learning and develop their own strategies and techniques, then they are likely to be more motivated to succeed. It is therefore important for maintaining motivation that learning tasks and experiences are always directed towards developing and increasing a student's experiences of success.

Stress, anxiety and distraction

If a learner has any concerns, however small they might seem, these can cause distraction.

We have all experienced how distractions can impede study, or anything we want to do that requires focus and concentration. In this context we do not mean unwanted noise or other distractions in the learner's immediate surroundings – although 'environmental' distractions of this kind can of course cause serious problems for some learners. Dealing with them is a case of trying to minimise them to an appropriate level, and we look at this in more detail in Chapter 12. Nor do we mean 'deliberate distraction' in the sense of taking a break from a project to focus on something else entirely. That is a technique that can be helpful in appropriate situations, and we explore it in Chapter 19.

What we are primarily concerned with here is a common problem that can have a powerful negative effect on learning – that of unwanted self-distraction. By this we mean those situations where a student wants to concentrate and is trying hard to do so, but his or her thoughts keep involuntarily straying away from the task in hand to other things. The important issue here is the extent to which the student is in control of his or her own ability to concentrate and study effectively.

There are ways of avoiding unwanted self-distraction, but first and foremost learners must feel good about themselves. Therefore, if someone has concerns or anxieties, there should be opportunities to talk about them. Stress can be associated with specific areas of school or academic work (an obvious example is exam stress, which we discuss more fully in Chapter 25), but more general life stresses affect learners at all ages, from early primary school through to university. Addressing these will not only benefit the learner in the short term, but also help with their long-term study practices.

Chapter 3: The learning environment

How the environment affects learning

It is well known that genetic factors can determine how the brain forms neural connections. What is less well understood is that how these connections work and are created in practice is largely determined by the environment within which learning takes place. This is crucial information because – unlike genetic factors – the environment can be adapted.

By the 'environment', we mean much more than immediate physical surroundings, although this of course can be problematic for some individuals and it is important to get it right. The term also encompasses the quality of the interactions between the student and his or her surroundings, and the wider social environment including the family, the school, the teacher and other students.

> **Key Point**
>
> *How the brain's neural connections work and are created in practice is largely determines by the environment within which learning takes place.*

The table overleaf gives an indication of the various ways in which different aspects of the learning environment can impact a learner and learning outcomes:

Table 1: Environmental determinants for learning

Social environment	Family	School	Teacher	Other students/ learners
Level and quality of resources available, e.g. appropriate materials, libraries	Level and depth of opportunities for conversation, addressing emotional needs and developing social skills	Level and quality of learning experiences	Level and extent of resources available and potential to adapt classroom layout	Level and extent of opportunities for positive interaction and the development of social skills
	Providing opportunities for decision-making and developing a sense of agency	Opportunities for experiencing success in a variety of areas and/or ways	Access to an appropriately varied and relevant curriculum	Developing a sense of belonging
		Type and range of resources available	Providing opportunities for interaction	Providing opportunities for problem-solving

A positive learning environment

It is important to ensure that there is always a positive learning environment, both in school and at home, as part of a broader approach to positive learning. Positive learning is important for developing the student's feeling of confidence in his or her own worth or abilities in relation to carrying out schoolwork successfully. It is easy to imagine the impact that a severe lack of academic self-esteem could have on the ability to learn – particularly when the subject area is challenging or the outcome is being measured. A positive learning environment is a key element of this.

> **Key Point**
>
> It is important to ensure that there is always a positive learning environment, both in school and at home.

At school, the drive for a positive learning environment must come from the top. Only when senior management and all staff are on board with a positive learning philosophy can a school ensure consistent commitment to helping all learners and those who work with them. As part of this, as we have noted, it is important to take a wide and holistic approach to the young person, to the styles of teaching, and to the physical environment in which the teaching and learning will take place.

A key point of positive learning relates to ownership. It is important that pupils have some vested interest in what they are learning, have opportunities to make choices, and feel that it is their own course of study and learning rather than one that has been imposed on them by the teacher or the school. This way, they will be more motivated to learn and, even more crucially, to succeed. It is always important for pupils to see learning as relevant to them. Setting up and adapting the environment to suit their strengths and needs helps with this sense of ownership.

Challenges related to the learning environment

Barriers to learning

The notion of 'barriers to learning' is vital, because it puts the focus on what might be preventing the child or young person from learning – as opposed to focusing on a learner's own possible difficulties or deficits. So it is important always to consider this overall perspective as a starting point when we are looking at how to help learners. Possible barriers include the time of day when learning, any undue stress and anxiety placed on the learner (for example, deadlines or word constraints), expectations, and how comfortable or otherwise the learner feels in relation to the learning environment. Some of these are discussed in more detail below, and in subsequent chapters.

> **Key Point**
>
> *It is important that pupils have some vested interest in what they are learning, have opportunities to make choices, and feel that it is their own course of study and learning.*

The school ethos

The school ethos describes the overall approach to education taken in the school as a whole. For it to be valued and applied throughout, it must be actively supported and promoted from top level. It should take account of challenges that face pupils in relation to personal and interpersonal and environmental issues, and of what we know about the learning process. The school's ethos should include attention to educational 'emotional literacy' – the ability and confidence of learners to access and talk about their feelings toward being in school and the subjects being taught.

Feedback

In order to ensure self-esteem and encourage positive learning, it is important for learners to receive positive feedback. This is not simply a case of telling them that they have done well. If we only ever did this, then the value of that feedback would be diminished and there would be the risk of patronising learners and/or failing to challenge them. Learners need to know what they have done well, how they did it well, and what areas (that are within their reach) they could work on to improve. General praise does not have the same value as specific praise!

Metacognition – understanding how you learn

Linked to the notion of feedback is an awareness of how important it is for a learner to have some understanding of how he or she learns best. Vygotsky differentiated between the 'cognitive' (learning how to do things) and the 'metacognitive' (understanding and controlling the process of learning).[3,4] He also highlighted the importance of being able to use metacognition to help with further, advanced learning. So learners don't just need to learn information – they also need to learn about themselves in relation to how they work best. This is a recurring theme in this book.

Expert View

"Learning is more than the acquisition of the ability to think; it is the acquisition of many specialised abilities for thinking about a variety of things."

Lev Vygotsky

Classroom design

Acknowledging that people learn differently also leads us to consider the physical environment of the classroom. This includes elements such as lighting, seating, and the amount and nature of sounds. Some consideration should be made of how these can be made adaptable for learners.

---

3   Vygotsky LS (1962) *Thought And Language*. Cambridge, Mass: MIT Press.
4   Vygotsky LS (1978) *Mind and Society: The Development Of Higher Psychological Processes*. Cambridge, MA: Harvard University Press.

Differentiation

It is very important that tasks are perceived by learners as achievable. To ensure this, the teacher needs to be able differentiate the materials and outcomes sufficiently so that each individual learner will be able to complete tasks successfully. Differentiating means offering a variety of ways of delivering the information, and a variety of ways of finding out what pupils have learned.

Chapter 4: The process of learning

The individual learner

Children and young people (and adults, for that matter) learn in a range of different ways. Some of us are very visual, others like to hear information out loud, others prefer the written word and still others must be physically engaged in order to maximise learning outcomes. Similarly, some people are able to work well alone and others do much better when they study in a group. Each one of us has a way in which we learn best, known as a learning style. As well as teaching curriculum materials, learners will usually need specific help with understanding the process of learning – that is, the different ways in which people can learn, and how they as individuals learn best.

> **Key Point**
>
> It is very important that the school as an organisation makes it a priority to teach pupils about the process of learning, because it is the foundation for successful study.

As we have indicated, a successful approach to planning learning must take a much broader and more holistic perspective than just focusing on an individual's internal thought processes. It should also give attention to organisation, time management, ways of learning and learning styles, investigative skills, how to retain and retrieve information, and how to reproduce information in the forms needed for success in exams and beyond. These topics are all discussed in detail in Parts 4 and 5.
It is very important that the school as an organisation makes it a priority to teach pupils about the process of learning, because it is the foundation for the successful study of curriculum subjects. This must be part of the school's wider ethos, because otherwise it is too easy to become engrossed, or bogged down, in subject areas and teaching to exams. Teachers need to know that they are supported in taking the time to work on this important 'metacognitive' perspective of learning.

Challenges related to the learning process

Time management and organisation

Time management and organisation can be an issue for individuals – particularly further up the school, when learners often complain about having too much homework or too many subjects in their timetable and not enough time to spend on study or other interests in their life. It is important to help young people formulate a set of priorities. Scheduling ahead can be difficult, but a study plan is essential for organising and coping with a heavy workload. It is also important for learners to set goals that can keep them motivated and give direction, and this applies across the age range. The goal must be achievable and realistic, but also stimulating and challenging; if it is too easy then it may result in under-achievement or even boredom, and the learner can 'switch off'. The balance between what is realistic and what is challenging is the crucial factor, and the teacher must have insight into the learner's style and preferences in order to achieve it and guide progress effectively.

Information-gathering

Researching and fact-finding are important skills for children and young people to learn from an early age, to help them take ownership of their studies and to promote independent learning. Across all subjects there will be scope for a range of information-gathering approaches, and which to use will depend on a number of factors including the individual's learning abilities and preferences. Reading is of course a fundamental method for discovering new information. It is therefore important to identify any difficulties that might hamper a child or young person when reading and decoding words, and to put in place any support that may be needed to help them learn.

Note-taking

Note-taking, or more broadly recording information that is being taught, is a vital skill for students, and it is surprising how often we find difficulties in this area. Some issues relate to the mechanical skills of handwriting or typing. Often, students find it hard to hold information in short-term memory long enough to write it down (memory is discussed in Chapter 21). Many of these difficulties can be addressed by using information technology. We should also consider what we know about students' learning styles, and the importance of linking new information to prior knowledge. This gives us a basis for helping learners to record information in a way that comes more naturally and makes sense to them. These are the kinds of notes that will genuinely help students to retain what they have learned.

Linking new information to prior knowledge

When we want to understand and absorb new information, it is absolutely vital to be able to link it to what we already know about a topic or subject area – however little that might seem to be at the start. Being able to access prior knowledge helps with learning and metacognition (this is discussed in more detail in Chapter 17). It develops children's understanding because it

> **Key Point**
>
> *Learning is not simply the ability to store, remember and recite facts. What is important is to be able to manipulate this information to answer questions.*

locates the information in a meaningful context, giving them something to 'hook' it on to. Doing this can also help with motivation, because the learner should be able to see why that new information is relevant.

Problem-solving skills

Learning is not simply the ability to store, remember and recite facts. What is important is to be able to manipulate this information to answer questions. That is the basis of real understanding and deep learning. Pupils who only learn to recite facts will soon find that this strategy has limited application. In exams, for example, they will be asked to compare, contrast or analyse information, and in Science or numerate subjects they will often need to figure out first which formulae or theories are relevant. So an element of problem-solving is crucial. There is a very positive side to problem-solving. It can clearly make learning more challenging, but it can also make it much more interesting and engaging because it can change dull repetition into an interesting puzzle to be tackled.

Understanding what is being taught

The key to success in learning does not depend on a good memory (although this is important, and will be discussed later), but rather on good understanding. Put simply, if the material is understood, it will more easily be retained. One of the ways to ensure understanding of a topic is for the student to self-question. Students will be able to learn more effectively and study more independently if they have a good understanding of the topic and can ask the right questions to gain further understanding. Self-questioning is a skill, and it should be explicitly taught.

Making subject teaching learner-friendly

Although much of what is taught at secondary level is pre-determined, this does not mean that teaching should not be as learner-friendly as possible. It can be argued that the fundamental principles for making information learner-friendly are the same across all subjects, and if teachers combine forward planning with curriculum differentiation and an understanding of how children learn then a learning programme can be achieved that is accessible and engaging for all students.

Supporting and improving memory

We all know that it is possible to come to class, pay attention, understand what is said at the time, take notes, and yet still find it very difficult to remember all the information we need to take in. We have noted above that students need an understanding of how they learn, and closely related to this is the need to understand how memory works, how to tell when it is not working (it isn't always obvious!), and the kinds of strategies that might help.

Active information processing

As the complexity and volume of academic work increases, strategies that make learning and retrieving information easier for students become invaluable. Through active processing techniques such as overlearning and mind maps, stress and anxiety can be kept at bay and study time can be made more efficient. These strategies can vary between learners and with the specific subject areas and topics that are being taught.

Specific challenges related to essay-writing, exams and lifelong learning

Planning and writing a good essay

The main reason for difficulties in essay-writing is that. for this task, you have to demonstrate expertise in a wide range of study skills, starting with reading and information-gathering from a range of sources, note-taking and organisation. In addition, you must show that you can translate all the ideas into accurate, continuous and preferably convincing prose. As with other aspects of study, organisation is a key feature of successful essay-writing, and more often than not it needs to be explicitly taught to students if they are to fully demonstrate their knowledge and ability.

Effective revision

When approaching the task of revising for exams, students should not allow the exam itself to become the focal point. What is important is to get the learning right, and the key to success here is organisation. With good organisation revision becomes manageable, learning becomes more engaging, understanding of issues is enhanced and success becomes more achievable. Revision is therefore best viewed from a perspective of learning strategies and learning skills.

Exam preparation

The very mention of the word 'exam' can invoke a great deal of stress in many students. Yet in reality it is an opportunity for the learner to show how much he or she knows, and it can be seen as 'pay-off' time for many hours spent preparing for the exam. Still, many well-prepared students seem to fall down when faced with an exam paper, and some of this is undoubtedly due to anxiety and exam stress. While a certain level of anxiety can be beneficial in some circumstances, higher levels can have a detrimental effect on performance and results. Managing anxiety, and identifying those who may be at risk, is therefore critical.

Sitting the exam

If revision and exam preparation has gone to plan, then the student should feel good entering the exam room. From here, the key challenge is to manage time and effort effectively in order to answer all the required questions in a manner that maximises the return on study time. Some exam questions unfortunately seem to be designed to trick students, and under pressure and exam stress a student can easily misinterpret the question. That is why being mentally prepared is important. It is also crucial to equip the student with test-taking skills to allow adequate time for reading and understanding the questions, as well as revisiting each question at various times during the crafting of his or her response. After the exam, it is important to relax and celebrate.

Lifelong learning

'Lifelong learning' has become something of a catchphrase in today's society. There is certainly an increased emphasis on lifelong learning and all its ramifications, and there are also more opportunities, and often requirements, to undertake 'on-the-job training' and Continuing Professional Development (CPD) in most occupations. It seems that nowadays no one can escape learning! This can also mean studying and exams. For many older adults who have been away from school for a lengthy period, this can cause some issues, particularly if they have had a job change or job promotion and have new tasks to master. Very likely they did not receive a course in learning skills at school!

Ten key things to know about study and learning

1. As well as studying subjects and topic areas, it is crucial that pupils learn how to learn.

2. Learning is an active process – it is not simply memorising information.

3. We need to consider the role of self-esteem, self-confidence, stress and anxiety in successful study and learning.

4. Motivation is a key factor in successful study and learning.

5. Individuals learn differently, and it is very important for pupils to be shown how to explore and examine what works for them.

6. Different ways of learning must be reflected in the ways that individual pupils are taught, and in the ways in which they are assessed.

7. Strategies for particular types of study and learning (for example, exam techniques) can and should be explicitly taught.

8. Positive, differentiated learning strategies should be used school-wide and for this they need to be fully supported at management level.

9. Wider, societal factors are important for learning, including access to resources and opportunities for discussion, engagement and representation.

10. Learning is a lifelong skill – it's something that we need throughout our lives.

Part 2: Personal and interpersonal issues

Chapter 5: Self-efficacy and self-esteem

Positive self-esteem is crucial for learning, because a positive perspective on learning can provide the learner with the confidence and motivation that are needed to draw on the widest range of approaches that can reinforce learning. The following table gives some indication of the general characteristics of positive and negative self-esteem:

Table 2: Factors that affect self-esteem

Positive self-esteem	Negative self-esteem
Positive attention	Ignoring the person
Praise	Criticism
Respect	Not respecting the person's views
Friendships	Loneliness
Success	Failure

More specifically, in relation to education, positive self-esteem gives the learner the confidence to take a risk with learning, and with studying strategies. A learner with negative self-esteem will likely have a cautious approach to learning, and will be over-reliant on the structure provided by the teacher, or the teaching materials. It is unlikely that such learners will develop a high 'metacognitive awareness' because they will not have the confidence to become responsible for their own learning. Metacognitive awareness relates to the student's knowledge of how he or she learns best. It is crucial that students assume responsibility for their own learning, and this can be a long and gradual process that will continue throughout their education. They need to develop their own structures and strategies and eventually gain the skill of being able to assess, evaluate and improve their own competencies in different tasks.

> **Key Point**
>
> *It is crucial that students assume responsibility for their own learning, and this can be a long and gradual process that will continue throughout their education.*

We will draw on the characteristics noted in Table 2 above to show ways that parents, carers, teachers and schools can boost the self-esteem of learners. It is also extremely important to encourage the learner to take some responsibility for developing his or her own self-image in a positive way. This will allow the learner to accept and adapt to the different

> **Key Point**
>
> The experience of success cannot be over-estimated. It is important to look for ways in which success can become a reality.

challenges he or she will face over time, to feel secure in the learning experience, and to take credit for success. The experience of success cannot be over-estimated. It can help learners with low self-esteem to believe that they can do a task. It will also increase motivation. It is important to look for ways in which success can become a reality. This may not always be easy, and often one has to review what is actually meant by success. This depends a great deal on the expectations placed on the learner either by him- or herself, or by others. The important point is that the learner needs to recognise that he or she has been successful.

How to help – self-efficacy and self-esteem

☞ **Attention**

- **Recognise the individual** – it is important to value the learner as an individual. Using names is important, especially in High School, where a teacher can see several hundred children in one week. If the child is valued as an individual, then he or she will begin to appreciate that, and this can have an impact on the child's feelings of self-worth and self-esteem.

- **Display the child's work** – this can have a really positive impact on some children. Work should be displayed as much as possible, and it is very important not to favour the same cohort of pupils when doing so.

☞ Praise

- **Identify strengths** – children will begin to believe in themselves if they are able to utilise their strengths. This will give them positive reinforcement, and help to generate motivation as well as positive self-esteem.

- **Positive communication with parents** – there is a great deal of research showing the impact of parents' views and beliefs on their children (see, for example, Pomerantz, Kim and Cheung [2012],[5] Le Mare [2014],[6] Gonid and Cortina [2014][7]). In terms of 'significant others', the parents rank at the top for most children. It is crucial that a positive message about the child is given to parents. This will transfer to the pupil.

- **Focus on the positive** – it is widely accepted that most children (and adults) will respond better to an acknowledgement of what they are doing well than to punishment or negative comments that focus on their mistakes. So, start by trying to find the positive, even (in fact, especially!) if this is hard. Finding something positive gives you a 'way in' to develop the learner's confidence and trust.

- **Ensure tasks are achievable** – if the learner repeatedly fails tasks, then this will lower motivation and consequently affect self-esteem. Try to avoid providing tasks that are ambiguous or too demanding. Take account of the strengths you have identified in that learner.

- **Be real** – your praise has to be sincere if it is to be valued. Learners, particularly those who struggle with negative self-esteem, can find it hard to accept praise and they have to be able to believe the praise they are given (even if it takes time and some repetition). It is easier to give genuine praise if you have made the task achievable, as noted above.

- **Be constructive** about areas that need to improve and be specific about how this could be achieved.

---

5   Pomerantz EM, Kim EM & Cheung CS (2012) *Parents' Involvement In Children's Learning* in Harris KR, Graham S, Urdan T, Graham S, Royer JM & Zeidner M (Eds) *APA Educational Psychology Handbook, Vol 2: Individual Differences And Cultural And Contextual Factors*. Washington, DC, US: American Psychological Association.
6   Le Mare L (2014) *How Does Parent Involvement In Education Affect Children's Learning?* Available at: https://www.edcan.ca/articles/the-facts-on-education-how-does-parent-involvement-in-education-affect-childrens-learning/ [last accessed 16 January 2021]
7   Gonida EN & Cortina KS (2014) Parental involvement in homework: Relations with parent and student achievement-related motivational beliefs and achievement. *Br J Educ Psychol* **84**: 376–96.

☞ Respect

- **Responsibility** – develop the child's self-respect by trusting him or her with responsibility for some aspects of classroom duties or organisation. For example, a younger child might be asked to be in charge of the pens or some other duty that is manageable for him or her. Be careful in choosing situations where this can be done, so that the pupil feels respected and valued, and not patronised or put-upon.

- **Peer approval** – what others in the class think of a child is very important to that child. Children need approval, and approval and friendship from peers is likely to be more influential than from adults. It is important therefore to ensure that the class is aware of the needs of others, and can consider the need to be positive and respectful towards other children in the class. This can be done in a general way – for example, by raising awareness of the different ways that people learn and different ways that they can best demonstrate their learning.

☞ Friendships

- **Being part of a group** – this can work to the learner's advantage if the group dynamics are positive. It is therefore important to take time to ensure the composition of the group is favourable for each learner, and to monitor this over time.

- **Playground buddies** – peer group friendships are important to all children. A system of playground or classroom buddies can have a spin-off effect on pupils' classroom work and motivation to study. It can be helpful to all parties – it can improve the confidence and self-esteem of the child who provides the guidance, and give the child who is being 'buddied' some support and role-modelling.

☞ Success

- **If you have planned for success, you will find it** – if you have made tasks achievable (as noted above), you should be introducing the child to the experience of success.
- **Success does not have to be in school work** – there are plenty of other areas of development seen in the school that can be just as valuable in life, including working in groups, encouraging others, creative and sports achievements.
- **Celebrate success** – this is important, because it can give the learner a real sense of achievement. Acknowledgement of success should be appropriate to the task and the level of the student – so that it is valued, and appreciated by the recipient.

Chapter 6: Motivation

When we consider motivation, it is important to think about where we can find or produce it. Certainly, teachers, parents, carers and others can be motivating. We can probably all think of an example of someone who inspired us to try something new, or to push ourselves that bit harder. We all know, too, that we can have the best of intentions to follow that inspiration, but we also need to have a real, personal commitment to stick with it. Attribution theory (Heider, 1958) provides a useful starting point for understanding more about this.[8]

Expert View

"Man is usually not content simply to register the observables that surround him; he needs to refer them as far as possible to the invariances of his environment."

Fritz Heider

The basis of attribution theory is that we have a natural tendency to look for explanations for things that happen to us and around us. It can be quite uncomfortable to think that we have no idea why things happen, and understanding – or attributing a cause – can give us some sense of control. Heider suggested that one of the most important motivating factors in people's lives is the sense they make of their perceived successes and failures. The theory suggests that people can attribute their actions, successes and failures to either internal reasons (that is, due to the individual) or external (due to outside forces or influences). Attribution theory has been explored and developed over the years. Weiner (1972) drew on the theory to understand how our attributions might affect our future actions, and in particular our motivation.[9]

What is important, then, is how much the student attributes success or failure to internal causes or external factors. We have seen in the previous section how important the feeling of success is to self-esteem and self-confidence. If that success is attributed to the teacher, or to another member of the group, or to a book or resource that he or she was using, then the student can't take credit for that success and future success will be seen as dependent on these external factors – not under the individual's control. Similarly, if the student fails at the task, he or she could blame that failure on others, or on external circumstances.

---

8   Heider F (1958) *The Psychology Of Interpersonal Relations*. New York: Wiley.
9   Weiner B (1972) Attribution theory, achievement motivation, and the educational process. *Rev Educ Res* 2(2): 203-15.

If students experience some difficulty with a task – for example, a Mathematics problem – they may see the outcome as fixed and out of their control, decide they 'cannot do Maths', and give up.

So, we can see how students may come to believe that some outcomes are controllable or uncontrollable and, as a result, that some outcomes are changeable or fixed. If we believed that the outcome was going to be the same no matter what we did, and that the outcome was definitely not going to be good, would we feel like trying? Sometimes an apparent lack of motivation is in fact a strategy to avoid what is thought of as inevitable failure. The student might not be actively thinking this, but that can be the effect of his or her attributional perspective.

Expert View

"Internal versus external control refers to the degree to which persons expect that an outcome is contingent on their own behaviour or characteristics versus a function of chance, luck, or fate."

Julian Rotter

Rotter (1966) further explored issues of control and similarly categorised them as 'internal' and 'external'.[10] Drawing on this theory, some students may think they are doing badly because they are not bright enough, or because they aren't working hard enough, and this would reflect an 'internal locus of control' or the tendency to take personal responsibility. Alternatively, they might think their difficulties are due to poor teaching (suggesting an 'external locus of control' or the tendency to see responsibility elsewhere). They may see themselves as capable of developing their learning skills by hard work (internally controllable) or they may see themselves as simply unable to learn, however hard they try (uncontrollable because the control is external to the student). This latter example, sometimes described as 'learned helplessness', can be a destructive influence on the student's self-esteem.

Attribution theory therefore relates to how much responsibility the student takes for success or for failure. It's a fine balance, because this will rarely be due solely to that person's abilities or effort – external factors, and luck, can play important parts in both. However, if we want students to take an active role in their learning, we need them to take control of it. This can pave the way for the further development of self-esteem. It can also promote independence, and more confident learning, better success and ultimately improved motivation for future work.

---

10   Rotter JB (1966) Generalised expectancies for internal versus external control of reinforcement. *Psychol Monog* 80(1): 1–28.

Ideally, then, motivation should be intrinsic, because this will help the learner to become self-motivating. We know that if students experience repeated failure it is de-motivating, and this helps us to understand more clearly what can be done to motivate (or re-motivate) learners – early success is very important when tackling new tasks. Intrinsic motivation can, however, help students take control over their learning. For intrinsic motivation, students need to:

Key Point

If we want students to take an active role in their learning, we need them to take control of it.

- enjoy the learning experience
- have an appetite for learning
- be inquisitive
- understand what they are learning
- be able to see new learning as part of a bigger picture

If the student is to enjoy the learning experience, he or she has to have some experience of success. Success builds on success, and early and significant success is an important factor when new material is being learned. To create and develop an appetite for learning, the child must over time become an independent thinker. This is also important because it helps to promote independent decision-making and helps the student come to conclusions without too much direction from the teacher. This active and enquiring approach to learning will help with understanding, and it will help the learner to locate what they learn in the wider context. It can also help to develop confidence in a learner, and help to motivate the learner to tackle new material. As we will see in the rest of this book, it is also important that both extrinsic (rewards) and intrinsic (self-motivation) factors are considered in the planning of learning, and many of the above points will be revisited and discussed in greater detail.

How to help – motivation

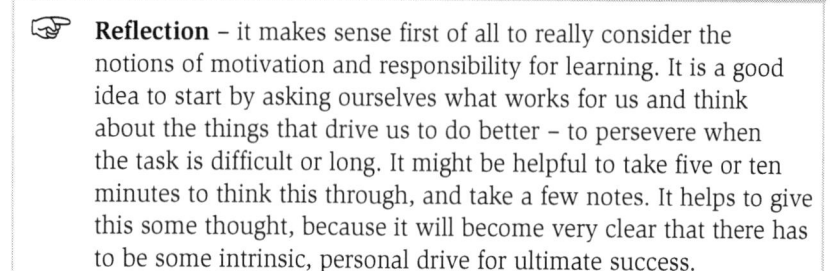

☞ **Reflection** – it makes sense first of all to really consider the notions of motivation and responsibility for learning. It is a good idea to start by asking ourselves what works for us and think about the things that drive us to do better – to persevere when the task is difficult or long. It might be helpful to take five or ten minutes to think this through, and take a few notes. It helps to give this some thought, because it will become very clear that there has to be some intrinsic, personal drive for ultimate success.

☞ **Discussion** – taking your own experiences and perspectives as a starting point, try to find out what really motivates the learner you are working with. Ask some questions about natural preferences:
- What topics, tasks and activities interest the child?
    - What topics does the child speak about confidently?
    - What is it about these tasks, activities and topics that attract the child?

☞ **Persistence** – does the child find it easy to stick with a task when it is something he or she enjoys? What happens when the task is difficult?
- Does the child stick with a task until completion without breaks?
- Are frequent breaks necessary when working on difficult tasks?
- What is the quality of the child's work with and without breaks?
- What kinds of prompting are necessary to keep the child on task?

☞ **Responsibility** – does the child take responsibility for his or her own learning?
- Does the child attribute successes and failures to him- or herself, or to others?
- Does the child see a relationship between effort put in, and results achieved?

☞ **Incentives** – ask about the kinds of rewards that might be valued by that child:
- Does the child seem to work because of an interest in learning, or to please others – e.g. parents, teachers, friends?

- What type of incentives motivate the child – e.g. leadership opportunities, working with others, gold stars, free time, physical activity?

☞ **Ensure that tasks are felt to be achievable** – how this is done will vary according to the task, the subject and the age and stage of the learner. The following example of motivating younger children to read illustrates the underlying principles you should keep in mind.

If reading is challenging for children, it is likely they will switch off from reading. One way of dealing with this is to provide 'hi-lo' books – that is, books that are high in interest but low in vocabulary demands. These books can help with fluency, comprehension and motivation to read. Specifically, the hi-lo books from Barrington Stoke can be useful (www.barringtonstoke.co.uk). These books have accessible layouts and spacing to ensure that the page is not overcrowded. They use heavier paper with a slight tint to help reduce visual stress. They are also edited to ensure unnecessary words don't hinder comprehension, although the text and stories will still be challenging for the reader. Crucially, the content is matched to the age of the reader, not to his or her reading level. This can be motivating.

Taking these steps can engage the learner in books. When reading is more enjoyable, the child will read more, which will improve his or her reading and increase enjoyment of text. This can pave the way for self-learning and eventually self-study. In 2019, Bloomsbury Publications published JK Rowling's *Hogwarts* books in a user-friendly font and style, and these can also be motivating: (https://www.bloomsbury.com/uk/fantastic-beasts-and-where-to-find-them-9781408894590/).

☞ **Ensure that tasks are felt to be appropriately challenging** – don't confuse lack of motivation with lack of ability. Students will often lack motivation if the work they have been given is unfulfilling. This can account for lower exam results than expected, and it can be a particular challenge when working with gifted students. It is important to bear that in mind when investigating why a learner is showing a lack of motivation.

Insights from students

The following quotes came from senior students who had recently taken important examinations (Lucas, 2002)[11]:

"The grades that I was expected to get were around borderline pass/fail, yet I actually achieved four passes all in the top grades. The reason for the predictions being so low was probably based on the fact that I do not learn well in the classroom environment. The teachers therefore did not realise what I was capable of because my progress in class lessons had not been good.

I found my own way of studying. I was motivated because I wanted to go to a good university and to study the course that I wanted. I found it best to spend four hours each day on my own in the library, write my notes out in full and then summarise them until finally I reached the stage when I could fit the large paragraphs that I had summarised on to one line! When all my notes were complete, I read them every night in the build-up to my exams, and the result was that I did a lot better than even I was hoping for. Now I will be able to use this strategy again, and I will be even better at using it next time." (Stephen, aged 17 years)

This is an interesting response, because the student realised it was up to him. He took responsibility for his own learning, and it paid off. Furthermore, the student had intrinsic motivation. He identified his own goal – a place at a good university – and therefore he was not dependent on external rewards. The incentive came from him. This helped the student to identify and appreciate the best way of learning for him. Additionally, having used the strategy, Stephen now believes he will be able to use it again.

Stephen's methods of studying (four hours in the library) contrasts with Ruairdh, who said that the best way for him was to *"sit down, put on some music, make sure I am completely relaxed and work for twenty to thirty minutes. I would then stay in the same place, but do something quite different like leisurely reading for about ten minutes"*.

Another student, Mark, found that his best strategy was practice and repetition, with rest breaks. He uses 'write' and 'check' techniques to learn vocabulary. He said: *"When revising, I get bored so I do it in small*

---

11   Lucas S (2002) Personal correspondence in Reid G (2005) *Dyslexia And Inclusion: Classroom Approaches for Assessment, Teaching and Learning.* London: NASEN/ David Fulton.

bursts, having a small break in the middle. Then I go back to see if the revision has had any effect."

The above students do seem to be using an auditory type of strategy, which of course is not suitable for all. Rose, aged 17, said: *"I am a very visual person, so I remember diagrams and mental images though visual strategies. I know this because I used the example in English Literature from the play* Romeo and Juliet *as being like a 'lightning bolt'. I found it incredibly useful to have a visual image to associate with a scene or play."* Rose has developed visual approaches to understanding and remembering information, but again the important point is that she decided on the approach herself and practised using it as she felt comfortable with it.

Another student, Bronte, said: *"I find that I only need to be taught an outline of the subject so that I can sort it into some sort of structure in my brain. The only way I can pick up detailed knowledge is to sit down on my own for long periods of time and write out detailed, structured notes with mind maps. I'm very much the kind of person who has to write facts out lots of times to learn them! If I can't see a logical sequence in a subject, I find it very difficult to take on board – it is important to me to see the whole picture before I can start to concentrate on the smaller bits."*

Bronte provides a good example of a learner who uses analytic, auditory approaches and visual and global approaches. She needs structure, needs to write things out and has to learn through knowing the logical sequence of events. This is an analytic and auditory type of approach, yet Bronte also needs to use mind maps to see the visual images and to make the connections. Importantly, she also needs to have an overview of the whole picture of what she is studying. This tends to be a global (seeing the patterns between elements), right-brained (creative) type of approach.

How to help – learning preferences

☞ The findings of the research study discussed above emphasise the importance of students deciding for themselves on their learning preferences and styles. The senior students involved had all been introduced to study skills throughout their time at school, and it was therefore relatively easy for them to identify the most appropriate methods and experiment with them. It is important that students are allowed to do this and given encouragement to find the best style for them. The younger this process starts the better.

☞ Other approaches and strategies that were indicated most strongly in the research were:

- use of highlighters
- use of spider diagrams
- placing 'Post-it' notes around the room
- listening to music
- using small note or index cards
- writing notes in bright colours
- using audio books

Chapter 7: Stress and anxiety

It is important to help learners feel good about the learning challenges they face – from completing classwork and homework to taking class tests and exams. This can partly be achieved by encouraging them to reflect on their feelings and to discuss them with a trusted person.

> **Key Point**
>
> The more the learner feels a sense of control over his or her learning, the less room there is for stress and anxiety to take a hold.

A recurring theme in relation to successful learning is the need for some feeling of control. The more the learner feels a sense of control over his or her learning, the less room there is for stress and anxiety to take a hold. The best thing clearly would be to avoid these feelings in the first place, and much of what is proposed in this book is aimed at creating the conditions where the learner does feel a sense of responsibility and that learning tasks are achievable, interesting and fulfilling. However, there will be pressure points in the course of any learner's school or academic career, and it is important to prepare for this, from an early age.

It is therefore important for learners to realise they need to *prepare* for challenging learning. It is a good idea to introduce learners to a range of different relaxation techniques but it is best to keep this simple, so that they can use the approach when they are on their own, at home or in other contexts. Music can be helpful, and many learners will naturally turn to this to help them wind down. However, relaxation should not just be seen as something that happens in the background.

Just like learning, it helps if the student takes an active role in finding the things that work for him or her and putting that knowledge into action. For example, it is important that they make sure they take, make or create dedicated time for relaxation, which can be as important as actual time spent on studying. It is important that learners receive that message and, if it is embedded at an early stage, it is more likely that they will have developed techniques and strategies that work for them. These will then be built into their everyday approach to learning – not just added in at times of high pressure when relaxing seems the hardest thing, and sometimes even an indulgence if time is tight.

How to help – relaxation

Relaxation techniques should be taught from a young age, so that they become second nature to the learner in later years. The following procedure can be used:

☞ Preparation

- Ensure that all items that may be distracting are out of sight
- If relaxation is to take place in the classroom, ensure the desks are cleared
- If the relaxation activity involves music and visualisation, it is best to dim the lights as this will minimise distraction and aid visualisation
- If you are giving instructions, speak in a softer voice than usual
- When coming out of the relaxation period, increase the volume of your voice slowly and gradually break off the relaxation time.

☞ Techniques

- Eyes closed, listening to relaxing music
- Visualisation techniques – imagine a scene such as a beach or holiday destination
- Free time – allowing time for a favourite activity, without any form of structure or demands
- Exercises involving body flexing, such as yoga and stretching
- Games and sports
- Puzzles – word searches, colouring in activities.

It is a good idea to ask the student to think about his or her own preferred relaxation techniques. This also demonstrates to them that the same technique may not work for everyone, so it is okay for them to have their own preferred techniques.

☞ Scheduling

The value of regular and varied relaxation can be reinforced by asking students to make a timetable just as they might produce a revision schedule. In fact, it could be incorporated into that schedule to demonstrate that this is just as important in terms of that person's happiness and sense of achievement. It's worth reminding students who say they just don't have the time to relax that thinking this way actually means that they need to relax!

Relaxation	Time	Activity
Monday		
Tuesday		
Wednesday		
Thursday		
Friday		
Saturday		
Sunday		

Part 3: The learning environment

Chapter 8: Barriers to learning

In the previous section, we emphasised how valuable it is for the pupil to take responsibility for his or her learning. The other side of this coin is that we, as parents, carers or teachers, need to take responsibility for providing the context in which different children will thrive, and this means reflecting carefully on what we can do to enable this for all learners.

Key Point

It is important that learners of all ages are able to identify the barriers that may be preventing them from accessing new learning.

It is also important that learners of all ages are able to identify the barriers that may be preventing them from accessing new learning. Earlier chapters have discussed the role and the importance of interpersonal and interpersonal issues for learning – self-efficacy and self-esteem, motivation, and stress and anxiety. These need to be considered at the outset. But it is important to see the learner in the context of the wider environment, and within that environment there are other factors that can act as barriers to successful learning.

In terms of interpersonal issues, we have seen that it is important that the task is within the learner's comfort zone (but not too easy), in that he or she feels it is both achievable and interesting. So, if the level and scale of the task aren't right, this could be a barrier to learning. We need to create conditions in which stress and anxiety can be discussed and alleviated. Apart from the actual task, the learner can experience challenges in areas such as attention, memory and confidence. These can prevent the learner from developing his or her full learning potential, so we need to consider these as potential barriers when we are looking at ways of developing learning and study skills.

What we would like to stress here is that it is important to acknowledge that there may be barriers that are stopping the learner from reaching his or her potential. It is a way of thinking that can prevent us from focusing solely on the child's difficulties. We have seen so many times that children are described as 'easily distracted', 'lacking in motivation', 'disorganised' or just lacking in ability. These descriptions may hold some truth, but they just tell us what is happening on the surface – the outcome of a range of factors that might be affecting that learner in that particular task or subject area.

For example, one of the dynamic and growth areas in the learning literature is in the field of accelerated learning – that is, using the brain more efficiently to learn more effectively. There is a growing body of research on the brain, and with magnetic imaging techniques it is now easier to understand and explain how the brain works. Three key areas are of particular relevance for learning: characteristics, capacity and connections:

- **Characteristics** – the learning characteristics of the individual, i.e. his or her learning preferences and how they can use them, is important. Each student will have a learning preference, but it is important each student is in a positive learning environment to ensure he or she can access these preferences effectively.
- **Capacity** – all brains are capable of learning. We need to look for 'trigger points' to help with association – one trigger point can lead to other points – and building up associations is the key.
- **Connections** – brain cells (neurons) are constantly changing and making new connections with other cells and groups of cells. There will be trillions of connections at any one time, but some of these connections will become redundant if they are not used and others will become stronger with learning. Edelman (1992) discusses the theory of 'neuronal group selection', which indicates that groups of neural circuits become specialised – for example, some deal with emotions, some with social situations and others with sensory processing.[12] If young children are deprived of practice in social situations, then they will become less competent in these situations because they will not have the neural connections to support learning and behaviour in this context. Learning is therefore about exposure to language, and a rich learning environment.

---

12 Edelman GM (1992) *Bright Air, Brilliant Fire: On the Matter of the Mind*. New York: Basic Books.

We believe it is helpful to always be open to the possibility that there might be barriers preventing that child from fully participating and benefiting from learning. If we take this perspective, then it becomes important to explore these issues with the learner. This will help us to move to the next steps of reducing those barriers.

How to help – barriers to learning

☞ **Reflection** – try to put yourself in the learner's shoes. It might help to observe the child while he or she is involved in a learning activity. Ask yourself a few questions:

- What do you know about his or her talents and interests? Are they reflected in the work that is being produced?
- Is the child having difficulties in some areas, but not in others? If so, why might that be?

☞ **Discussion** – speak to the learner, and do this in a non-confrontational way. Take time to ask him or her:

- What subjects do you find easier, or more interesting?
- What do you think it is about these subjects that makes them easier, or more interesting?
- How do you think you work best?
- What is it about the other subjects that makes them harder, or less interesting?
- Do you have any concerns about your progress, or about anything else?
- If so, what do you think might help?

Chapter 9: The school ethos

Effective learning should be seen as a whole-school initiative and therefore the principles of positive learning should be a priority in staff development, so that staff feel supported and validated in the widest aspects of their role. From a high level, there should be policies and support for addressing personal and interpersonal aspects of learning – self-efficacy and self-esteem, motivation, and stress and anxiety,

Key Point

It is important that the school management does everything that is reasonably possible to ensure that the school is learner-friendly.

and factors that relate more directly to the learning environment and the learning process (these are discussed more fully in the rest of the book).

It is important that the school management does everything that is reasonably possible to ensure that the school is learner-friendly and conducive to children becoming self-sufficient and effective learners. The ethos of the school needs to be supportive in creating a positive learning environment. Staff development is important because the school ethos involves the whole staff, and they need to feel confident that they understand and can implement the philosophy and perspectives embedded in the school ethos in the course of their day-to-day work.

One of the most useful learning styles models is that developed by Dunn, Dunn and Price (1992-1993).[13, 14] This model identifies five principal domains containing 21 elements, all of which affect student learning:

- **emotional** (motivation, persistence, responsibility, structure)
- **environmental** (sound, light, temperature, design)
- **sociological** (learning independently, in pairs, with peers, in a team, with an adult)
- **physiological** (perceptual preference, food and drink intake, time of day, mobility)
- **psychological** (global or analytic preferences, impulsive and reflective)

---

13 Dunn R & Dunn KJ (1992) *Teaching Elementary Students Through Their Individual Learning Styles: Practical Approaches For Grades 3–6.* Boston: Allyn & Bacon.
14 Dunn RS & Dunn KJ (1993) *Teaching Secondary Students Through Their Individual Learning Styles: Practical Approaches For Grades 7–12.* Englewood, NJ: Prentice Hall.

These domains take account of personal and interpersonal issues, and the learning environment. The concept of 'emotional literacy' is important because it helps learners feel more aware of their needs and the needs of others. It can help with successful studying because it can make the student feel more able to study, and more able to persist with challenging material. Emotional literacy can be linked to emotional intelligence. Both relate to the capacity in individuals (and groups) to perceive, understand and manage emotions in relation to the self, and in relation to others. Learning takes place in the wider context of the school, and this means that emotional learning has to be fully absorbed and fully included in the whole-school ethos. This is important because it is often the case that emotional problems underlie some of the behavioural and learning problems that can be seen in the classroom.

There are five pathways to emotional intelligence – self-awareness, self-regulation, motivation, empathy and social competence. These are all necessary for the development of emotional wellbeing and emotional literacy.

Key Point

There has to be a clear focus on the learning process as well as the subject matter that has to be learned.

There also has to be a clear focus on the learning process – that is, how students learn – as well as the subject matter that has to be learned. This is important if schools are to make the curriculum accessible to all learners. A well-constructed learning skills programme can enhance confidence and autonomy in the learner, metacognitive awareness (an understanding of how the child learns best), understanding, recall and demonstration of acquired knowledge. It is important to bear in mind that the development of learning skills does not need to be subject-specific. It can be easier to teach skills by using a subject area as an example, but they should be very much presented as generic, so that the learner can transfer them to other topic areas.

Learning skills programmes will vary with the age and stage of the learner. A programme for primary children would differ from one designed to help students cope with examinations at secondary level. Well-developed study skills habits at the primary stage, however, can provide a sound foundation for tackling new material in secondary school, and help equip the student for exams. One of the key issues in relation to successful study in secondary school concerns the notion of responsibility for learning. It is important to ensure that children develop independence to equip them for independent study in further and higher education and, indeed, in the workplace. Learning is for life and the 'how to' should have its roots at school.

How to help – embedding a positive school ethos

☞ **Communication** – the philosophy of the school and its Mission Statement (or equivalent) needs to be clear and accessible to teachers, parents and carers, and students.

☞ **Staff development** – staff will need support and training so that they can apply the school ethos in practice, in the different aspects of their work with pupils. Workshops can provide opportunities to air concerns about the pace and the nature of the students' learning experiences and the staff's teaching role in development work, planning and teaching. It is important that staff workshops to address the needs of the whole school to enhance effective learning are seen as an important element in school training. Some key points that should be considered in staff development include:

- how to help all pupils to become confident, active and independent learners
- an awareness of methods of preventing and dealing with stress and anxiety
- the need to value all students and staff
- how to improve the learning experience for all learners

☞ **Parental collaboration** – this needs to be considered and seen as a priority. Parents are a very rich source of information and assistance, and it is important that ongoing collaboration between home and school is encouraged.

☞ **Comprehensiveness** – the ethos should draw on the many perspectives of positive learning, i.e. the personal and interpersonal, and on those relating to the school environment, and it should be informed by what we know about the learning process.

☞ **Emotional literacy** – it is important that schools have an ethos that encourages and develops emotional literacy. This can, for example, include specific policies on bullying, or on supporting teachers and pupils experiencing stress. It could include regular opportunities to discuss issues such as motivation, communication between pupils and interpersonal skills, through circle time or in scheduled sessions, and the incorporation of these topics as part of discussions that might arise more spontaneously.

☞ **Learning skills programme** – a specific learning skills programme will provide a framework that ensures that an ethos of positive learning is embedded and followed.

☞ **Review** – there should be routes open for discussing and potentially changing elements of the school ethos (for example, how it is to be put into practice) to take full account of the valuable experience of the different stakeholders.

Chapter 10: Feedback

Feedback is crucial to maintain motivation and extend the learner's challenges. Ideally, it should be provided continuously throughout a task, as well as at the end of the task. That way, the pupil will know if he or she is going down the wrong track, and will be able to avoid putting a lot of effort into something that is likely to lead to failure. So, the timing of feedback is important.

Key Point

Feedback should be seen as a learning opportunity, in that it can teach pupils to self-monitor so that eventually they evaluate their own work as part of the learning process.

The type of feedback is also important. If it is to be useful to the pupil, it should be practical, based on achievable outcomes, and constructive. That way, the pupil will know what to do to improve his or her work, or approach to learning.

Finally, feedback should in itself be seen as a learning opportunity, in that it can teach pupils to self-monitor so that eventually they will evaluate their own work as part of the learning process, and in a way that does not discourage or de-motivate them. This means they will be able to figure out for themselves where they might be able to make improvements, and take positive steps that will improve their outcomes.

How to help – positive feedback

☞ **Positive reinforcement** – it is important to start feedback with positive comments, and then some points for development can be mentioned. Some positive comments should also be made at the end of any feedback session.

☞ **Guidance** – the key point of any feedback is to provide the learner with guidance to ensure that he or she can progress towards achieving the task. It is not helpful just to be told that something 'could be better'; some pointers need to be provided to show the pupil how this might be achieved. Guidance can and should be framed in a positive way to help to maintain motivation.

☞ **Suggestions for further work** – it is also important that the learner is left with a framework and suggestions for future development. This could be specifically related to the task – for example, further reading or additional resources that could be accessed. It could also be more generic, and this will help the learner to apply the principles of the feedback to other areas. For example, there might be some discussion of how the pupil could structure his or her answer better to answer the question that was set. This kind of advice will definitely be applicable across a wide range of subject areas, and it would be useful to make this explicit to the learner.

☞ **Self-assessment** – the key point of this is to attempt to empower learners sufficiently so that they can take on the responsibility of monitoring, evaluating and improving their own work. This addresses the need for learners to gain some control over their own learning, which (as we have seen) is important for intrinsic motivation. It is also a skill that becomes increasingly important as the learner moves up the school, and in later learning.

Chapter 11: Metacognition – understanding how you learn

Learners need to develop an understanding of how they learn because there are many of ways of absorbing, understanding and retaining information. Knowledge of one's learning styles and preferences is one of the keys to successful learning and self-sufficiency in learning.

> **Key Point**
>
> *Knowledge of one's learning styles and preferences is one of the keys to successful learning and self-sufficiency in learning.*

It is important to recognise that different children and indeed adults will have their own preferred learning style. Learning preferences incorporate the whole learning experience. They can include factors relating to the individual, such as information processing skills, and can also relate to whether the learning is done by working in groups or in pairs, or indeed whether the learner works better on his or her own. They can also include environmental factors such as time of day, type of light, background music, level of noise and the type of seating arrangement. These are discussed more fully in Chapter 12.

Although traditionally there has been a greater emphasis on certain types of teaching and learning, we now know that many children slip through the net because these particular methods don't work well for them. So, we need first of all to consider the different ways in which different individuals learn best. That means there needs to be some consideration of:

- **the cognitive area** – that is how students process information, through visual, auditory, tactile or kinaesthetic means
- **social learning** – whether they prefer to learn on their own or with others
- **environmental preferences** – this means the type of classroom layout, desks, light and sound in the learning environment, as all of these can have some impact. Some learners prefer a quiet, no-noise environment whereas others prefer a noisy background, and some need to have music on while working.

Given and Reid (2005)[15] noted there are at least 100 instruments designed to identify individual learning styles. A study by Coffield et al (2004) identified 70 learning styles instruments.[16] We can see from this that there is a great variety of descriptions of learning styles. Reid (2005) notes that these instruments usually focus on a number of key factors that are seen to be influential in the learning process.[17] These include:

Expert View

"When teachers understand how the brain's learning systems function, they teach more effectively while gaining more joy in teaching."

Barbara Given

- modality preference – that is, a preference for a form of input that is visual, auditory, tactual or kinaesthetic
- personality types – such as intuitive, risk-taking, cautious and reflective
- social variables – for example, a preference for working alone or with others
- cognitive processes – including memory, comprehension and methods of information processing
- movement and laterality – such as a preference for active learning, and left- and right-hemispheric activities.

Given (2002) developed a comprehensive approach to learning styles by incorporating five 'learning systems', which will be associated with different 'learning goals'.[18] The learning systems are matched to learning goals, as shown in Table 3 below:

---

15 Given B & Reid G (2005) *Interactive Observation Learning Styles*. Edinburgh, UK: University of Edinburgh.
16 Coffield F, Moseley D, Hall E & Ecclestone K (2004) *Should We Be Using Learning Styles? What Research Has To Say To Practice*. London: Learning and Skills Research Centre.
17 Reid G (2005) *Learning Styles And Inclusion*. London: Sage Publications.
18 Given BK (2002) *Teaching To The Brain's Natural Learning Systems*. Alexandria, VA: ASCD (Association for Supervision and Curriculum Development).

Table 3: Learning systems and learning goals

Learning system	Learning goal
Emotional	Self-direction
Social	Self-assurance
Cognitive	Self-regulation
Physical	Self-control
Reflective	Self-assessment

Given argues that learning systems may be guided by the genetic code, but are also subject to environmental input for their detailed patterns and responses to different learning situations. The key therefore is the interplay between the pupil and the context of learning. It is important, according to Given, that we recognise the importance of this interplay and are able to use pupils' natural learning systems to help them to develop educationally.[18]

It should be acknowledged that those factors, and all styles of learning are mediated by:

- **the learner's culture** – that includes goals, motivation, availability of learning materials and the place and status of learning in that culture.
- **the classroom and school climate** – the learner needs to feel that he or she fits into the school, and feels comfortable learning in that environment.
- **teaching style** – the role of the teacher, and specifically the style of teacher, have an influence on all learners.
- **expectations** – the learner must feel that the task is achievable, and may need to be shown how to achieve a particular task. It may therefore be necessary to change and adapt the expectations. If the expectations are too high, the learner can become de-motivated; if they are too low, he or she can become bored. It is a question of balance, and this is very important.

It's also important to remember that, although we will each have some general preferences for learning, it can often be helpful to draw on a variety of methods to sustain interest, motivation and success. Carey (2015) argues that routine is not useful for successful study but that, on the contrary, variety is more important.[19] For example, he suggests that changing locations can help to take advantage of the 'context effect' in learning. The context effect describes the finding that we are more likely to remember information if we put ourselves back in the same context where we learned it. This is the principle that is used, for example, when police stage reconstructions. They are hoping that this will trigger memory for information and details that otherwise would be forgotten. If we want to draw on this principle, we could instead try to imagine ourselves back in the environment we were in when we studied it. It could be confusing if all our studying was done in the same environment, and changing it – perhaps strategically, to suit the subject – could provide us with better contextual cues or triggers.

When pupils really understand how they learn best, they are more able to take control and, as we have seen in earlier chapters, this can help with confidence and it can help to reduce stress and anxiety. Having this knowledge helps the learner to take more responsibility for his or her progress, and to be able to work more independently. Successful learning can depend on this. It is too easy for learners to take a passive role, and for teachers to take control and, sometimes inadvertently, direct the student's learning. Many students flounder when they reach College or University because they have been too dependent on a teacher.

Expert View

"If the brain is a learning machine then it's an eccentric one. And it performs best when it's quirks are exploited."

Benedict Carey

One of the strategies for developing learner independence is to develop metacognitive awareness, and the confidence to take some control over their learning. That is not to say they need to use their learning preferences all the time; they will need to be able to learn, and work, in a number of different learning situations. However, if they have this self-knowledge, and know their learning preferences, they can revert to them when they are facing a demanding task. If the environment does not allow this then at least the learner will have some understanding of the impact this might have had on performance.

---

19 Carey B (2015) *How We Learn: The Surprising Truth About When, Where, And Why It Happens*. New York, NY: Random House Trade Paperbacks.

The degree of independence a learner can acquire over tasks can have an impact on the outcome. Learners who have this independence can often use their existing knowledge and skills to tackle other tasks in other learning situations. In other words, they are able to transfer their skills to new learning. So, the development of metacognitive awareness enables the student to transfer what he or she has learned to future studies, and this is a skill that will be useful beyond school and in general aspects of future life.

Metacognitive awareness produces learners who:

- are efficient and successful
- have some appreciation of their own learning preference because this knowledge can help to make learning more efficient
- ask themselves *how* they arrived at a particular response
- are able to understand the information they needed to obtain that response
- are aware of which strategies were successful, and which were not
- are knowledgeable about how they could use specific strategies to tackle future problems.

If we are to encourage pupils to understand how they learn best, and to use this information to improves success and develop independence, we need to consider how they can:

- **explore and experiment** with different learning styles
- **develop self-knowledge** in relation to their learning preferences
- **direct** their learning
- **monitor** the learning experience
- **assess** the results of their learning **and evaluate** the learning experience
- **transfer** this learning/knowledge to new learning situation.

The following strategies can be used to develop these skills.

How to help – understanding how you learn

☞ **Exploring learning styles**

It is important that the teacher or tutor has an awareness of what is meant by 'learning styles' and how to identify different styles in learners. Teachers, parents and carers can help by taking time and care in observing the pupil, then discussing what they have found with him or her. It is important to acknowledge that there might be differences of opinion here, because different perspectives are being taken. However, it can provide a starting point, and encourage the pupil to progress to self-observation and towards greater awareness of his or her natural preferences. Given and Reid (2005) have developed a framework that is flexible and adaptable, and can be used in natural settings with interactive activities – the Interactive Observational Style Identification (IOSI) (see Appendix 2 for a summary of this).[15] A framework such as the IOSI can be used as a guide and perhaps be supplemented by more formal measures of learning style.

We believe that for learning and teaching it is beneficial to use some form of identification for learning 'preferences', even if it may not be a precise or infallible measure. The following activity can help teachers, parents and carers to understand the pupil's motivational preferences in relation to the learning environment. Knowing this can be important, particularly if the student is tackling a challenging task. For each item, ask the pupil to circle the option that is best for him or her. Younger children could have the questions read out to them, or pictures could be used to describe the different situations in the questions. Some students may need some explanation for each of the questions, and this is okay:

- I prefer to learn… in the early morning, late morning, afternoon, late at night
- I prefer to work… at a desk, on the floor, lying on a cushion, at a table
- I prefer it when the room is… cold, cool, warm, very warm

- I prefer to work... with a dim table light, with bright, overhead lights, in natural light
- When I work, I need... silence, some background noise, background music, a lot of noise
- When I am working in class, I prefer to... sit still, move a lot around the class, move around a little, move around only occasionally
- When I am working, I prefer to... talk with someone, not talk at all, talk only occasionally
- I do/don't like a lot of space around me in the classroom
- I like to work at my own desk and workspace/to share a workspace with other people
- I like/don't like to learn visually
- I like/don't like to learn by listening to someone
- I like/don't like to make or do something when I am learning
- When I am given a new task... I like to take time to think about it before starting/I prefer to get started straight away.

It is important to consult with pupils over the responses. (We have used the term responses rather than results, because we want to stress that there is no right or wrong answer.) It is vitally important to communicate this to the student – that is, that there are no right or wrong answers.

Discuss what the results may mean in terms of the students' study pattern and show how they might be able to incorporate their responses into their class work and independent study. This is an important part of the exercise. The implications of most of the responses to the questions are self-explanatory, and it is important to help the student work out how they use these responses in their learning plan.

One of the key aspects to consider is the potential to provide the learner with choice, because it is only by trying out different methods that the learner will be able to discover how he or she works best. Modalities of learning, classroom design and differentiation are discussed more fully in the remaining chapters of Part 2.

☞ **Developing self-knowledge**

Encourage self-questioning, which is a key factor in understanding a task and responding correctly to tasks – for example, when taking on new learning, pupils should ask themselves:

- Have I done this before?
- How did I do it?
- Is this the best way to tackle this problem?
- What did I find easy?
- What was difficult?
- Why did I find it easy, or difficult?
- What did I learn?
- What do I have to do to accomplish this task?
- How should I tackle it?
- Should I tackle it the same way as before?

☞ **Direct, monitor, assess, evaluate and transfer knowledge of learning styles**

Every effort should be made to organise the learning environment in a manner that can be adapted to suit a range of styles to enable the pupil to direct his or her learning as appropriate. This means that the lighting, design and indeed the whole learning atmosphere need to be flexible. These are discussed in more detail in Chapter 12.

Chapter 12: Classroom design

The learning environment is perhaps one of the most underrated factors in the learning process. Frederickson and Cline (2002) note that there is substantial literature that supports the importance of the learning environment.[20] Environmental factors can account for differences in the development of learning skills, motivation, school attendance and examination performance.

> **Key Point**
>
> *A learning styles perspective that includes the learning environment can hold the key to helping all children learn effectively.*

Student attitude, as well as achievement, can be enhanced through paying careful attention to factors within the classroom environment. This indicates that the learning environment is crucial, particularly in relation to learners who may have difficulties in acclimatising to different teaching styles. Dockrell and McShane (1992) also suggest that the environment, and the interaction between the environment and the learner, are crucial – in addition to the tasks to be undertaken.[21] It is for that reason that a learning styles perspective that includes the learning environment, as well as a focus on the curriculum and teaching approaches, can hold the key to helping all children learn effectively.

Environmental factors can greatly increase or decrease the effectiveness of learning – but many learners are not aware of this, and often just accept the environment as it is without making any attempt to manipulate it in any way. Of course, this is more likely to be the case if they have not ever been exposed to alternative environments, or given any choice. If learners are aware of their environmental preferences, then they are in a position to make informed choices when they have some flexibility over learning.

The benefits of taking responsibility for learning have already been stressed. In most cases, certainly for younger learners, the learning environment refers to the classroom, but it can in fact refer to the other areas that are used for learning, such as the library, family and community settings. We should look at the learning environment as an important resource for helping to enable and empower learners to succeed.

---

20 Frederickson N & Cline T (2002) *Special Educational Needs, Inclusion and Diversity: A Text Book*. Buckingham, UK: Open University Press.
21 Dockrell J & McShane J (1992). *Children's Learning Difficulties: A Cognitive Approach*. Oxford: Blackwell.

There are a number of factors that need to be considered in relation to the learning environment. These relate to the following:

- **class layout** – design, personal space, presence of others
- **the visual environment** – colour, lighting, wall displays
- **the auditory environment** – classroom and background sounds.

As noted below, there is some overlap between these features. While it is difficult to cater for all the preferences of all the learners in the class, it is possible at least to be aware of these preferences and to attempt to introduce some flexibility so that it will be possible to accommodate to most learners some of the time.

Class layout

Some types of learners, particularly auditory learners, will prefer desks to be in a conventional layout, and will prefer sitting in an upright chair when learning. Others, particularly global, right-brained learners (thought to be more creative and artistic, and able to go beyond the details to see 'the bigger picture'), might prefer an informal classroom design, and may even want to sit on a cushion on the floor rather than an upright chair. It is therefore important to be flexible in the arrangement and the design of a classroom.

The visual environment

Light, and in particular natural light, can have a significant effect on people, and can help or restrict learning. The condition known as Seasonal Affective Disorder (SAD) can cause depression in some people during the winter months. It is postulated that melatonin, a sleep-related hormone secreted by the pineal gland in the brain, is linked to SAD. This hormone, which may cause symptoms of depression, is produced at increased levels in the dark. When the days are shorter and darker, the production of this hormone increases. It has also been suggested that the amount of both natural and artificial light available can have an impact on learning. Pupils might prefer bright lighting, or find it over-stimulating.

Colour is another important factor in learning, and particularly in motivation and mood. There has been some recent emphasis on colour therapy. The effect of colours on the health, mood, attention and general alertness of people has been well documented in the popular press and magazines. For example, it is claimed that colour therapy can balance and enhance the body's energy centres by using the seven colours of the light spectrum, and it is thought that this can help to stimulate the body's process. Colours can stimulate, subdue, elate or depress individuals.

It has for some time been suggested that certain colours can have specific impacts on humans (https://www.verywellmind.com/color-psychology-2795824). For example, blue light has a calming effect, and red light has a stimulating effect. Blue and red colours are considered at the two extremes, with yellow representing the midpoint. These are also the three principal colours in a rainbow. On this basis, it is claimed that colours and colour combinations have a profound effect on one's wellbeing and therefore it is not surprising that people might be affected by colour in a learning environment. Pastel colours are usually a 'safe bet', and these colours can be conducive to learning.

The auditory environment

People react differently to different sounds, and this needs to be considered in a learning environment. Some students will prefer a silent environment for concentration, Sound can be one of the most distracting elements in learning. At the same time, it has the potential to stimulate, invigorate and create. Some pupils may need some auditory stimuli, perhaps even music, in order to maximise concentration and performance.

> **Key Point**
>
> Sound can be one of the most distracting elements in learning. At the same time, it has the potential to stimulate, invigorate and create.

There has been a great deal of interest in the role of music in learning, both in terms of listening to music and in terms of actively playing a music instrument. For example, it has been suggested that children's educational, physical, and emotional development can be enhanced by soft music in the nursery, access to musical toys, dance lessons, and encouraging music involvement in a fun way.

It can be argued, therefore, that one of the best ways to enhance children's learning with music is to encourage listening to and learning music throughout the child's developmental years.

The term 'Mozart effect' was coined after a publication showing that students who listened to Mozart's *Sonata For Two Pianos In D Major* showed short-term subsequent enhancement of their spatial–temporal (ST) reasoning. Spatial–temporal reasoning describes the ability to think about and manipulate information in space and time. It is used in Maths and artificial intelligence to solve multi-step problems.

Research from the MIND (Medical Investigation of Neuro-developmental Disorders) Institute Research Division, affiliated with the University of California, Davis, discovered a link between music, the brain, and spatial reasoning. Additionally, Graziano, Peterson, and Shaw (1999), researchers from the MIND Institute, demonstrated that pre-school children given six months of piano keyboard lessons improved dramatically on spatial-temporal reasoning, whereas children in appropriate control groups did not improve.[22] It was then predicted that the enhanced spatial-temporal reasoning from piano keyboard training could lead to enhanced learning of specific math concepts, in particular proportional maths, which the researchers claim is notoriously difficult to teach using the usual language-analytic methods.

Overy et al (2003) also reported on the cognitive benefits of music training. They suggest that music training can be used as a multi-sensory medium for the development of timing skills, in which strong emphasis can be placed on analytical listening and accurate motor skills.[23]

How to help – classroom design

The classroom is essentially where learning takes place, and it is important that the learner feels comfortable in that environment. The layout of the classroom is important, and this includes the organisation of classroom furniture and the design of chairs and desks. Children need to be comfortable when they are learning, and what the environment looks and feels like are important. The colour scheme, lighting and how the space is used can all have an impact on the learner. It is important to note that teachers may have little control over some of these aspects, but it is important where possible to try to be flexible in the arrangement and the design of a classroom. This would mean that a number of different preferences could be accommodated. Ideally, classroom design should not be fixed and there should be scope for adaptations, depending on the preferences of the children in each class.

---

22 Graziano AB, Peterson M & Shaw GL (1999) Enhanced learning of proportional math through music training and spatial-temporal training. *Neurol Res* 21(2): 39–152.
23 Overy K, Nicolson RI, Fawcett AJ & Clarke EF (2003) Dyslexia and music: measuring musical timing skills. *Dyslexia: An International Journal of Research and Practice* 9(1): 18–36.

☞ School ethos

In Chapter 11, we stressed the importance of an understanding of learning styles. This should in fact be an influential feature in a school's daily practice, and in order for learning styles to be effectively implemented, this understanding needs to be incorporated into a whole-school ethos and policies. School ethos is discussed in more detail in Chapter 9. This will make it easier for individual teachers to incorporate learning styles into their daily teaching.

☞ Understanding learning preferences

It would be helpful for parents, carers and teachers to have some idea of the impact that the learning environment can have on individual pupils. This can be done by careful observation and discussion with the child.

☞ Class layout

In order for teachers to be able to accommodate different learning styles and preferences, classroom layout has to be made adaptable. For example, it may be necessary for the teacher to be able to change seating arrangements, or to provide students with a choice of desk styles. This will also enable different styles of interaction in the classroom, and can be used to facilitate individual study or groupwork.

☞ The visual environment

Some factors that can be considered include the following:

- wall displays
- the type of lighting in the classroom and the students' opportunities for changing the lighting to suit individual preferences
- colour schemes
- the size and the arrangement of the windows
- the outside view

In terms of wall displays, the level of stimulation must be considered – teachers need to ask themselves whether the classroom is over- or under-stimulating, and should try to achieve a balance between these. Too many bright or 'busy' displays can be distracting – but visual displays are also important; they can be stimulating and promote motivation and learning.

It might be possible to have softer lighting in some areas of the class, and this can be achieved by using desk or floor lamps – of course, bearing health and safety considerations in mind!

It may not be possible to give individual students choice over colour schemes, although if this possible their views should be taken into account. They could have some choice over the colour or tone of their own learning resources, and should be allowed to use their preferred colour whenever possible.

Windows and views cannot easily be changed, but their impact can be – for example, by the use of blinds, curtains or other screening.

☞ The auditory environment

Background music could be provided if this is helpful to the majority of learners, but for those who do not find it helpful, some alternative would need to be provided. This could be achieved by providing noise-cancelling earphones, which can also be offered to pupils who find the general background noise of the classroom to be distracting. It might be possible to create quiet zones within the class. This could be achieved by using carpets, bookcases, or plants, to create some level of sound-proofing. Some children might appreciate the opportunity to participate in musical activities, either as part of their curriculum or as a short 'time-out strategy.

Chapter 13: Differentiation

All teachers should be encouraged and, most importantly, supported to acknowledge and value the learning differences that will be evident in each classroom. Clearly, not all pupils will benefit from the more traditional 'oral instruction' form of teaching. As Barbe said: "If you've told a child a thousand times, and the child still has not learned, then it is not the child who is the slow learner" (Purkey, 1978).[24]

Expert View

"If you've told a child a thousand times, and the child still has not learned, then it is not the child who is the slow learner."

Walter Barbe

Accommodation of learning differences can be achieved through effective differentiation. This needs to be a reality to ensure that all children in the class will have an understanding of the topic, and be able to meet the learning targets of the class.

It is absolutely crucial to recognise and value creativity in our learners. This will develop and encourage interest, motivation and an active role in learning. These in turn help with understanding and recall (these are discussed more fully in Part 4). It is interesting to reflect on the view that many students can only develop their creativity *after* they leave school. Many in fact may fail at school. The pace of learning often seems to prioritise content, and ensures that all examinable areas of the curriculum are covered, but there may be less scope for digressing and for encouraging creativity. The examination system often does not reward creativity. Yet creative thinking can provide the learner with opportunities to develop his or her own style of reflecting and presenting information. It can also release the learner from the restrictions of following a process or sequence, perhaps suggested by the teacher or the textbook. Creative thinking for many learners can be a liberating experience. For some, this freedom to think creatively can be fun and invigorating and provide a vehicle for emotional expression and personal development.

The concept of 'multiple intelligences' is based on the view that there are many types of intelligence, including visual/spatial, verbal/linguistic, logical/mathematical, bodily/kinaesthetic, musical/rhythmic, interpersonal, intrapersonal and naturalistic. This concept can be drawn

---

24 Purkey W (1978) *Inviting School Success: A Self-Concept Approach To Teaching And Learning.* Belmont, CA: Wadsworth Publishing Company.

on to ensure that we consider a range of strategies to help the student access the full curriculum. As we have seen, learners will vary in the areas that come more naturally to them, and designing teaching and learning to suit the different types of intelligence will be useful for the wider range of pupils.

Parent, carers and teachers are often very aware of the fact that different people learn differently. As we have discussed in previous chapters, it is important that learners share this understanding, and that they know that it is okay – in fact, it is crucial – that they develop the awareness and confidence to ultimately be able to direct their own learning. It follows that if they are to be able to do this, they will need access to different types of teaching, different levels of support, and different ways of demonstrating what they have learned. So, teaching design, delivery and outcomes have to be considered.

One of the central points in developing positive learning is to try to simplify the ideas and the information as much as possible, so that the learning content and the tasks that are set are clear to pupils. This applies to learners at both ends of the learning spectrum – those who are very able, and those with marked learning challenges. The process and the principles of differentiation can provide a foothold to simplifying and clarifying information for all learners. It is also good practice for students themselves to utilise this strategy to help with understanding and retention, which means that good practice in the classroom can also have longer-term benefits for learners.

From the teacher's perspective, differentiation can be carried out by providing variation, based on individual pupils' needs, in relation to:

- tasks
- support
- outcomes

We appreciate that some of the strategies below might need to be adapted to fit into different classroom, teaching or home environments, but that is in itself one of the points that we are stressing in this book. It is important to be able to contextualise learning strategies for the work that is being done, and at the same time motivate learners to develop their own preferred strategies. Essentially, this is all about equipping the learner to carry out tasks in the best way for them. It is very important that learners are not only offered these different ways of working, but that over time they are encouraged to use the experience to differentiate for themselves.

The ultimate aim is always to boost students' self-esteem and to develop strategies that he or she can use independently, more widely across the school, and in later life.

It is useful if the teacher, parent or carer already has some understanding of the pupil's preferred learning style. This is discussed in Chapter 11. It is also worth noting that if a range of options is offered, this in itself can help to clarify what each pupil's learning preferences are.

How to help – differentiation

Differentiating by task

☞ **Encourage creativity** – this helps to develop thinking and problem-solving skills, and student responsibility. This can help students to take control over learning and encourage them to use their own ideas. For example:

- Rather than providing an essay title, provide the start of a story and ask students to finish it using their own ending. You could ask the students to complete a story from a prompt line such as: *and he said, "enough is enough!"*
- Provide an article or story without a title, and ask pupils to suggest an unusual title for the story. This provides a different angle on comprehension, and can make that task less daunting for some pupils.

☞ **Group work** – children should learn to work collaboratively with others, because this can be mutually beneficial. It can provide subtle support for weaker students, and it can help stronger students to clarify their understanding of a topic area. It is also a useful skill to develop. It is important to plan for group work. The dynamics of the group is crucial – everyone in the group needs to have a role to play. Working together should help students to recognise their own strengths and, importantly, to recognise the strengths in others. It can be useful to introduce group work from the 'supporting others' perspective. Each group member will have a responsibility to support one other member of the group. This underlines the fact that the group, although it is made up of individuals, needs to take on its own identity. This may not be easy, but with practice, each member of the group can become aware of the skills and the challenges of others in the group. It may be important to discuss this with the group before and after the task.

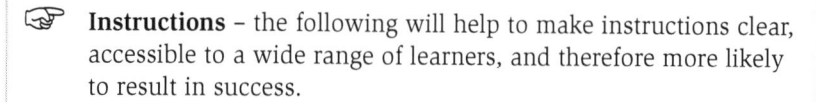

☞ **Instructions** – the following will help to make instructions clear, accessible to a wide range of learners, and therefore more likely to result in success.

- **break down information** – present it in smaller, manageable amounts. This can be done by using heading and sub-headings, in the form of bulletpoints, mind maps or 'spidergrams' (spider diagrams). (Spider diagrams are similar to mind maps. They start from a central topic area, and each sub-topic is related to the previous one in a system of nodes. Unlike mind maps, they rarely use colour or images.)
- **use different modalities** – add pictures to the text to aid comprehension, and/or read instructions out, one step at a time, to the student
- **provide, and highlight key words** or phrases (visually or verbally, e.g. by repetition); help learners to identify key points in a text
- **consider the accessibility of the task/content** – this could involve rewording using more simple vocabulary, and checking that sentences are clear, short and in a logical sequential order
- **produce a checklist** to ensure instructions have been understood, such as "What is actually being said/asked?"; "What is required of me?"; "How will I know if I am right?" Also, try to develop the student's ability to ask the right kind of questions about the task. Enquiry approaches can help to promote thinking skills.

☞ **Resources** – consider layout (using the same strategies for instructions, above) and the use of clearly labelled printed materials such as notes and maps to remove the need for lots of note-taking. Help learners to learn the skills of summarising information.

☞ **Achievability** – will the student succeed with task, or will it be too challenging? Is it possible for the student to investigate and find out more information without assistance? You might want to adapt the task to make the most of the strengths of the student, and/or graduate the task from simple to more complex.

☞ **Interest level** – will it hold the pupil's attention?

Differentiating through support

☞ **Learning environment** – consider how this is affecting the student (see Chapter 12 for more information on classroom design).

☞ **Visual presentation** – the following could be adapted for different learners:

- **font** – size, type and/or colour; for example, some people find it much easier to use a 'sans serif' font, such as Times New Roman, and find that black type is more difficult to read that coloured text.
- **paper** – coloured, plain, lined or squared might help according to the activity. Some learners find that white paper has too much glare. Lined paper can help with structure and neatness, but plain paper is better for learners who like to draw. Squared paper can make it easier to align numbers in maths or science tasks.
- **layout** – this is very important. It should be visually interesting, but not overcrowded.
- **visual aids** – many students will benefit from having a range of visual aids to support what they are learning. These can be in the form of photos, videos, pamphlets, brochures, or websites. It may be very helpful to have the student create their own visuals by drawing, colouring or painting.

☞ **Language support:**

- **vocabulary dictionary** – it may be necessary for students to use a personal vocabulary dictionary. This can be useful in at least two ways. First, it may save them the task of looking up the same word repeatedly if they cannot remember either the spelling or the definition. Second, it can help them when they are writing by having a handy list of descriptive vocabulary, synonyms for overused words (e.g. 'said' or 'nice') or words specific to an area of study.
- **picture dictionary** – it will really help some students to sketch a picture to represent the words in their personal dictionary. They may like to add colour where or when it is appropriate, or if time permits.
- **specialised vocabulary spelling lists** – this can be particularly important in technical and scientific subjects.
- **games** can be used to consolidate vocabulary.

☞ **Support in memory** – many students find it hard to complete tasks, simply because they have forgotten all of the task requirements, the information they need to know, or the steps needed to achieve success. Chapter 21 deals specifically with memory. The following strategies can be helpful:

- **Overlearning** – repeat and review information, using as wide a range of materials and strategies as possible (for example, mind mapping, colour-coding and mnemonics).
- **Link** new information to previous knowledge (this is discussed in more detail in Chapter 17), and show connections between different pieces of information – the learner may not be able to do this him- or herself.
- **Chunk** or group similar information to help learning to become more efficient.

☞ **Allow additional time** if necessary – the learner needs to complete the work as this will give him or her more satisfaction.

☞ **Information technology** – the learning skills of all students can be enriched through the use of technology and, most importantly, it can encourage and develop learner independence:

- 'Inspiration' encourages exploration and the understanding of words, mind mapping, numbers and concepts (http://www.inspiration.com/)
- 'Texthelp' can provide support for planning, organising and developing written work (https://www.texthelp.com/en-gb)
- Livescribe allows the learner to write notes, while at the same time recording everything. Tapping the Livescribe pen on a specially designed pad instantly starts audio recording. A specific part of the recording can be replayed by tapping the pen at that point in the notes. It therefore allows the student to take brief, bulletpoint or reminder notes, knowing that he or she will still have a full record to refer back to if necessary. All written work and audio recordings can then be transferred to computer. Any drawings, graphics etc are replicated exactly as they are on the pads. There are a range of pads, including A4, A5, notepad, and 'Post-it' notes. It is even possible to take notes in textbooks (www.livescribe.com/uk)

- The popular 'Clicker' programmes from Crick Software (www.cricksoft.com) can be used for sentence-building, word banks, writing frames and multimedia. It includes lively presentations – including, for example, a series on 'Find Out and Write About' that includes programmes on explorers, castles and animals. There are also Clicker books and Clicker animations.
- 'Co:Writer' provides vocabulary, spelling, composition and revision to support and build skills in writing (https://cowriter.com)
- 'Write Outloud' is a talking word processor – suitable for pupils aged eight or nine upwards (https://www.writeoutloud.net)
- 'PenFriend' is supportive writing software featuring word prediction (predictive typing), onscreen keyboards, a screen-reader speech feedback (http://www.penfriend.bis)
- Dragon 'Naturally Speaking' is a well-reviewed dictation programme that can type what the student says (https://www.nuance.com/en-gb/dragon.html)

Differentiating by outcomes

☞ **assessing attainment** – students could use a variety of methods to demonstrate their learning:

- in writing
- visually – using graphs, diagrams, mind-maps, etc
- verbally

☞ **consider mini-outcomes** – shorter, continual assessments can be less daunting, and provide students with the opportunity to gain confidence in their learning

☞ **self-monitoring** – are there opportunities for the student to self-monitor and self-correct? It is important that the learner is able to recognise and appreciate that he or she is making some kind of progression. A checklist can provide a useful way for the pupil to note and self-monitor his or her progress. A framework, or even a checklist, can help the learner to note and appreciate his or her progression:

Topic	What I already know	What I need to find out	Progress
The effects of climate change	Climate change in some countries	What is being done to prevent climate change?	Made a list of the actions being taken by different countries
		Why does climate change occur?	Made a list of the ways of slowing it down

☞ **be clear about expected outcomes** – the learner must know what the outcome of the task is supposed to look like

☞ **focusing on what is important** – understanding should be appropriately valued; details, e.g. of spelling and grammar, should be put in context

☞ **payback** – is there a reward at the end of the task, or is there some progression that the student will appreciate?

Multiple intelligence training

Lazear (1999) suggests that our education system, which has an emphasis on reasoning, can diminish the importance of imagination – often the imagination is very fertile in young children, but that can be lost in the shift to the importance of logic and reason as they progress through school.[25] He emphasises the importance of awakening the visual-spatial intelligence, and suggests that this can be developed in everyone. He suggests that visual-spatial skills can be developed through multiple intelligence training that can be integrated into the everyday class work. This can be done through exercises involving active imagination, creating patterns with coloured pencils and paper, through forming mental images and describing these, developing graphic representations and using perceptual puzzles in games (e.g. spotting similarities and differences).

---

25 Lazear D (1999) *Eight Ways Of Knowing: Teaching For Multiple Intelligences*. Arlington Heights, IL: SkyLight Training and Publishing.

Chapter 13: Differentiation

How to help – multiple intelligences

☞ **Drawing on multiple intelligences**

The 'multiple intelligences' approach can be used in all subjects, and to help make links between subjects. The figure below shows, as an example, how multiple intelligences could be used in Design Technology (Renaldi [2005], adapted with permission):[26]

Intelligence type	Characteristics	Practical applications and implications
Visual–spatial intelligence	Puzzle-building, understanding charts and graphs, sketching, painting, creating visual metaphors and analogies (perhaps through the visual arts), manipulating images, constructing, designing practical objects, interpreting visual images.	Designing and producing a folio; designing new concepts
Verbal/linguistic intelligence	Listening, speaking, writing, explaining	Orally explaining concepts or answers to questions; discussing in pairs/groups
Logical/mathematical intelligence	Ability to use reason, logic and numbers, performing complex mathematical calculations, working with geometric shapes	Working drawings; design concepts
Bodily/kinaesthetic intelligence	These learners express themselves through movement. Experiencing the physical process of a task enables them to remember and process information	Hands-on experience of practical tasks will provide excellent ways to remember manufacturing processes

---

26 Renaldi F (2005) *The Use Of Multiple Intelligence In The Classroom*. Perth and Kinross, UK: Kinross High School.

Intelligence type	Characteristics	Practical applications and implications
Musical/ rhythmic intelligence	Whistling, playing musical instruments, recognising tonal patterns, composing music, remembering melodies, understanding the structure and rhythm of music	Using a poem/rap to memorise facts can help jog the memory in an exam. An example of this could be a rhyme about the parts on a metal lathe
Interpersonal Intelligence	Seeing things from other perspectives (dual-perspective), co-operating with groups, noticing people's moods, motivations and intentions	Designing for specific target markets; seeking out business ventures as a game; launching new products
Intrapersonal intelligence	These learners try to understand their own inner feelings, strengths and weaknesses	Evaluating products, reviewing the specification and the quality of work; use a 'game show' approach to host a competition on new designs
Naturalistic intelligence	Studying in a natural setting, learning about how things work, categorising, preservation, conservation	Field work, nature study trips, YouTube videos showing how environmentally-friendly products can be used to replace current products

Part 4: The learning process

As we have discussed in Part 3, everyone has their own way of learning – and for that reason, the learning process can be very personal to the individual learner. Study skills books such as this, and study programmes, can help to provide guidance, impetus and hopefully inspiration, but the learner him- or herself must 'grasp the nettle' and develop personal and individual study and learning skills strategies. However, it will also help to have an understanding of the learning process, so that the learner can consider how he or she will best be able to meet the types of challenge that can be involved.

There is little doubt that teachers in today's schools are operating under a great deal of work pressures. Quite apart from the demanding role of teaching, they have to equip themselves with skills in administration and an understanding of testing procedures, learning differences, differentiation, resources, providing feedback to parents and keeping abreast of new educational initiatives and policies. This means that sometimes topics such as 'learning' and 'study skills' do not always receive the attention they warrant. The aim of this section of the book is to provide a detailed overview of how teachers can help children of all ages to develop learning skills that can promote learner independence. Ideally, learning and study skills should be integrated into everyday teaching.

There are a number of different theoretical perspectives on how children learn, and there are many competing views on learning strategies and how these strategies should be applied. The following are points of general importance:

- Intrinsic (within-child) factors as well as extrinsic, (environmental) factors can influence learning – we have discussed this in Part 2.
- Learning is a process that involves skills in organisational, information-gathering and note-taking.
- Learning is more effective when the content is familiar – this allows learners to develop creativity in their learning, and to fully understand and remember what they are taught.
- Learning is lifelong – this will be discussed in Chapter 27.

In this section, we focus on what is known about the learning process, and how to make it more effective. We specifically discuss the following aspects:

- time management and organisation
- information-gathering

- note-taking
- linking new information to prior knowledge
- problem-solving skills
- understanding what is being taught
- supporting and improving memory

Chapter 14: Time management and organisation

Inevitably, there will be more information and tasks to complete than students have time for. In all walks of life, people have to practice time management. It is important to discuss this with learners – even young pupils – because it is never too early to help them to organise how they plan to use their time.

> **Key Point**
>
> *Organising our time and creating a plan can give us a sense of control.*

When we believe that a task might be difficult, we can all have a tendency to put it off, in the hope that it will go away. Even the task of organising ourselves can seem a bit daunting, because it brings us nearer to the point of tackling what needs to be done. It is worth remembering, though, that organising our time and creating a plan can give us a sense of control. In fact, when people have very little control over how they manage their time, that can be even more stressful than taking responsibility for it. Research on assembly-line workers has shown that a lack of autonomy is linked to low work reward, and occupational stress (Ji et al, 2016).[27] So, although it can be a difficult thing to do, it is better to take charge of time management than to leave it in the hands of someone else!

Learning is a process, and it requires a period of consolidation. This has to be incorporated into planning and organising. 'Overlearning' is often necessary. Some learners may appear to have learned something new, but they may not have consolidated that new piece of learning. This means that they require a period of overlearning in order to ensure they have automaticity in the use of that new learning.

The following are useful considerations for time management:

- **Awareness** that time has to be used more efficiently – this is the motivation part of time management. It is very important because students have to see a need to be organised, and want to be organised, to use their time as efficiently as possible.
- **Planning** – deciding what needs to be done will need practice.

---

27 Ji Y, Li S & Wang C et al (2016) Occupational stress in assembly line workers in electronics manufacturing service and related influencing factors. *Zhonghua Lao Dong Wei Sheng Zhi Ye Bing Za Zhi* 34: 737–41.

- **Organising** what needs to be done.
- **Action** – doing what needs to be done.
- **Self-monitoring** what is being done is important for developing independent learning.
- **Evaluating** what has been done can help to make learning more efficient, and help the student to be able to use effective strategies for new learning.

How to help – time management and organisation

☞ **Awareness** – all students need an understanding of how they learn, and this will include an awareness of what their needs are and how to accommodate them. For example, overlearning can be essential for some students, and it needs to be planned. Students who know that they find it hard to stay focused on task will have learned that setting targets can help minimise distraction – because the focus moves to the target, and away from the learner! Metacognitive awareness is discussed more fully in Chapter 11.

☞ **Planning** – the teacher can start this process by giving the student a template of a plan, and asking them to complete it. When learners make up plans, it is important to spend time with them to go over the plans carefully to ensure the plans are comfortably manageable. Very often, learners can be too ambitious about what can be achieved in a given time. This can be counter-productive, and they can end up scrapping the plan altogether. The plan has to be realistic.

It can be useful to use the 'SMART' method. That is, the goals should be Specific, Measurable, Attainable, Relevant and Timely (SMART). A specific goal states exactly what the student plans to do – for example, not just 'work harder' or 'improve', but get at least 10 out of 20 in the next Maths test. That goal is also measurable, which is important because the learner needs to know whether or not the goal has been met. There has been much discussion of the need for tasks to be attainable, or achievable. This is what builds success, and confidence. 'Timely' means that there should be a timeframe for the goal to be completed. Planning will involve some prioritising of time and, when doing this, it is a goodidea to advise pupils or students to focus first on what they can do! This gives them confidence, and allows them to try out different ways of studying. By the time they get to the demanding materials or subjects, they may find it is less formidable than they first thought. As an analogy, it is like a football team scoring an early goal – it raises their spirits and raises their game to a higher level!

☞ **Organising** what needs to be done could involve making a 'to-do' list. Using colour and patterns can make this a fun activity for students. Most students will have access to a phone, and this makes it easy to set reminders and alerts. At a more general level, it is a good idea to get used to using an organiser of some kind. It doesn't have to be elaborate, but students do need one (and only the one!). They need to keep a note of what they have studied and perhaps a key sentence on the implications/importance of what they have studied. Although this seems to be geared to older students, this not necessarily the case; even younger, primary-aged students should be encouraged to do this.

It is worth exploring the many Apps that are available to help with organisation. For example, 'myHomework' is a useful scheduling and organisational app that is available both online, and as an app for smartphone platforms like iOS and Android. There are three icons on the homepage – 'Calendar', 'Homework' and 'Class Profiles'. Students can record their class information, build schedules, list assignments, and tie them all together with a calendar that marks due dates and class times (https://myhomeworkapp.com).

☞ **Action** – doing what needs to be done is the 'action' part and the student may need some initial support with this. A checklist can be used to keep track of what has been done, and the tasks that are still remaining. Time of day is an important consideration when planning; some learners can learn more effectively at certain times, e.g. morning, afternoon or evening. This can be particularly useful for planning weekends, when learners often have more choice over when to study. Remember that time should be allocated for relaxation and other activities!

☞ **Self-monitoring** – all the way through the learning process, students should be encouraged to ask themselves questions such as "How can I do this more effectively?" and "How can I use my time more efficiently?" They can be encouraged to do this by a supportive adult.

☞ **Evaluating** – Organisation and time management has to be seen in itself as a learning process. That is, students can improve their skills here if they spend some time evaluating how effective their planning has been. Was the plan achievable? Were the goals useful ones?

Chapter 15: Information-gathering

Gathering information and researching a topic is a vital skill in education, and one that pupils should start to learn from an early age. There are many different ways of doing this, and the best approach will depend on a number of factors – principally relating to the pupil's preferred learning approach, and the subject area. Learning styles and preferences are discussed more fully in Chapter 11. Some subjects lend themselves more easily to

Key Point

Reading is a primary way of learning new information. It is therefore important to establish whether or not pupils have difficulties that might affect their ability to read and decode words.

multikinaesthetic methods (that is, methods that use a range of senses, including auditory, visual and tactile). However, in all subjects there will be some room for using a variety of approaches to information-gathering.

It is important to help learners become aware of the processes they are using and, crucially, why they elected to use a particular approach. It is important to encourage them to do this on their own, so that they develop the skills of independent learning that will be needed throughout their education, and in later life.

Reading tends to be one of the primary ways of learning new information. It is therefore important to establish whether or not pupils have difficulties that might affect their ability to read and decode words. In addition, research shows that reading is much more than recognising and decoding words, and that intonation and emphasis are crucial if the pupil is to read for *meaning* (Davies, 1986).[28] Many young children will learn this instinctively – it is thought that by the age of two-and-a-half, most speakers of English as a first language will understand how these are used in speech. However, some pupils will find this difficult, and they will need additional support if they are to fully access the written word.

It is important to have systems in place to pick up potential reading difficulties as early as possible in a child's education. It's also worth noting that it is never too late to identify and support students with learning difficulties. It is important to have screening for dyslexia and

---

28 Davies M (1986) *Literacy And Intonation* in Couture B (Ed) Functional Approaches To Writing: Research Perspectives. Norwood, NJ: Ablex.

other Specific Learning Difficulties (SpLDs) available at different ages and stages of learning. In terms of reading for meaning, as noted earlier, an understanding of intonation and emphasis is crucial. This can be picked up through opportunities for conversation, and it can be encouraged by reading to very young children, and reading with them as soon as they are able to follow text at the same time (Davies, 2020).[29]

How to help – information gathering

☞ **Investigative process** – we need to make sure that pupils give some thought to which approaches might work best for them and for the task, by following the following steps:

- First, it is crucial that the student understands the task, so time should be spent in checking this. Don't miss out this step!
- Make a note of what the task involves. This could be in the form of a checklist or, for more visual learners, a mind map. Mind maps are discussed more fully in Chapter 22.
- Now, the student must take some time to think about what he or she already knows. The importance of referring to previous knowledge is stressed in Chapter 17 – essentially, this will help with understanding the new information to be learned. But at this stage it can help the student to be clear about what he or she needs to find out. Where are the gaps in his or her knowledge?
- Next, where will the student find the information needed to fill these gaps? Will it be available in their textbooks? In audiobooks? On websites? Students will often need some assistance in finding their way round their school, College or University Library, so that they can find printed information by subject or author. Learners can obtain a considerable amount of information from the Internet. But, at the same time, they can waste a great deal of time browsing and getting nowhere! It is important that they can locate one or two key websites, and focus on these. For some learners, using YouTube videos or similar can be very effective. It can be helpful when first using these techniques for the teacher or

---

29 Davies M (2020) *Reading For Meaning: Presentation At Scottish Parliament Cross-Party Group On Dyslexia, 15 Jan 2020.* Available at: https://www.parliament.scot/CrossPartyGroups/Session5CrossPartyGroup/Minutes/Dyslexia_20200115.pdf [last accessed 15 January 2021]

adult to help learners to structure their investigative process. This can be done by providing them with some key questions on what to look for. The students can then tailor their investigation to these questions.

☞ **Reading to learn** – when researching a topic, it is important to avoid reading for reading's sake. We can convince ourselves that we have researched a topic because we have spent a while reading about it. However, the task is not to read, but to learn something from the reading. It is good practice, after every paragraph or perhaps every two paragraphs, for students to note down a response to the question "What have I learned from this section?". If they do this after each section of the reading, they will have built up a personal picture of the text. It might also be useful to re-read the text, to confirm and reinforce the points they have noted.

This is a good preparation for critical reading and practising what is known as 'critical literacy' or 'inferential reading' – essentially, reading 'between the lines' and being aware that what the writer is actually saying may only be part of the meaning that can be drawn from that text. For example, it sometimes helps if the student can find out some background information about the author. What are the author's views? Does he or she have a particular point to make? Is the author likely to be biased in favour of one view or another? What has the author not mentioned? This emphasises that reading the text is a first stage in understanding, and that questioning and evaluation should be built into the reading exercise. This also makes it a more active process, and there's no doubt that this makes studying more interesting as well as more rewarding.

☞ **Indexes** – if your student is going to be looking for something specific in a resource, then it is good to train the him or her to locate and use the index or glossary. These techniques can be practised, as they can also help with the identification and highlighting of key points. Some other suggestions include:
- try to work out what you want to obtain from the text in advance
- develop a rough outline of the text, so that you know its 'geography' – where the different elements are located
- the headings in a chapter will help to build up a picture of the content

- look at different sections before reading the main body of the text – that is, start with the 'big picture' e.g. contents, index, chapter summaries. You don't have to start a book at the beginning!
- read short pieces of text, rather than lengthy pieces. It is helpful to break down a lengthy article or chapter into shorter sections
- make a note of key words and issues
- list any significant people or places
- use summary notes, and colour-coded key points (note-taking is discussed more fully in Chapter 16)

Reading strategies

Some learners can be easily intimidated by the quantity of reading they will have to do. It is a good idea to help them with some efficient reading strategies such as skimming and scanning. This means they are only reading the key points, which can be helpful if they have some background understanding of the topic and have a vast quantity of materials to read. Skimming means reading quickly to get the main idea of a sentence, paragraph, page or even a chapter or article. They can start practising this by underlining the key words. By skimming, they will be able to read quickly to get a general idea of a text so that they can decide whether it has useful information for them. Skimming can help to make their reading time more efficient.

You can skim by reading the first and last sentence of each paragraph. That can often give you an idea of what the paragraph is about. When skimming, it is important not to try to read every word. Skimming differs from scanning, in that when skimming you read across the way, and when scanning you read down the page. You would use scanning if you were looking for particular key words or names or dates. Most students will benefit from practice in scanning and skimming – reading to obtain a general overview or impression of the text. One way to practise scanning is to give the learners a passage to read, but not give them sufficient time to read the passage. This means they will be forced to read only the key words.

How to help – scanning text

☞ **Scanning passage – write five key points**

Ask your students to practice scanning the passage below, and writing five key points about the passage – and time them!

> ### Schema Development
>
> The development of schemas helps the learner organise and categorise information. It also ensures the utilisation of background knowledge. This can aid comprehension and recall.
>
> When learners read a story or a passage, they need to relate this to their existing framework of knowledge – i.e. their own schema. So, when coming across new knowledge, learners try to fit it into their existing framework of knowledge based on previous learning, which is the schema they possess for that topic or piece of information. It is important for the teacher to find out how developed a learner's schema is on a particular topic, before providing more and new information. Being aware of this will help the teacher ensure the child develops appropriate understanding of the new information.

Chapter 16: Note-taking

For many students, note-taking can be quite challenging, and time-consuming. Some may know that they will not even look at those notes again and, if they do, they may not understand what they mean. It is a good idea to spend some time with students assisting them in acquiring efficient note-taking skills.

Methods of note-taking

Students need to practise taking notes in a variety of ways to find out what suits them best. There are a variety of methods students can use, including bulletpoints, visuals, writing sentences, recording information and transcribing it later, summarising at the end of the piece/lesson and using technology. Often, handwriting is the most convenient way for short notes. If typing speeds are good, then the student may be able to produce notes on a laptop. This can be very useful, because they can more easily be added to or edited later. It can be useful to use a template for written notes, and this should start with the time and date, and the topic area. This will make it easier to locate these notes at a later date.

> **Key Point**
>
> Students need to practise taking notes in a variety of ways to find out what suits them best.

Sometimes, working memory difficulties can affect the pupil's abilities to take notes and this is discussed more fully in Chapter 21. College or university students are given permission to make an audio-recording in class. It is very important while doing this to still try to take some form of notes, even short, bulletpoints. This keeps the student actively engaged while listening, and it provides an outline for him or her to refer to in order to see which parts of the recording might need to be listened to again. Listening through all of the recordings would mean that student took at least twice as long to cover the course, and this is not always practicable. Livescribe is described in Chapter 13 on differentiation. It allows the learner to write notes, while at the same time recording everything. Tapping the Livescribe pen on a specially designed pad instantly starts audio recording. A specific part of the recording can be replayed by tapping the pen at that point in the notes. (www.livescribe.com/uk)

Students might also want to create their own audio notes from written texts. This is helpful for those students who do not have time to write notes, or who would rather listen than read. This can work for any topic or subject. They could use their phones to record themselves, perhaps reading the notes they have made, or some key points from the text book. It is a good idea if, after listening to the recording, to go through the key points mentally to ensure they have been learned.

There is also a range of software that can be used to help learners to get their notes down in writing, including CoWriter (https://cowriter.com), Notability (https://www.gingerlabs.com/), Read&Write Texthelp (https://www.gingerlabs.com/) and Dragon Naturally Speaking (https://www.nuance.com/en-gb/dragon.html).

Other strategies that can be relevant for note-taking include:

- Electronic notes can be provided by the teacher with questions and spaces for the student to elaborate on these.
- The student can also use a digital recorder to dictate their own notes and then write them up later.
- The student can write summaries of chapters and books and discuss these with the teacher.
- The teacher can give the student a framework with spaces for the student to elaborate. This can also help the student with organisation of the information. For example, in history a timeline can be helpful.

Structure

It is useful to start with a skeleton plan of what will be covered in class. Handouts can be very useful, especially if they can be provided before a class, so that the student has an opportunity to read them in advance. The handouts should provide a skeleton of the topic area. Sometimes the teacher can provide typed notes on the topic, but while this may be very useful it can short-circuit the learning and enquiry process for some students. There is more likelihood of the information being more effectively learned if learners actively write their own notes. Simply reading other people's notes may not be too helpful, so ideally handouts should just provide the outline and there should be space for the student to add his or her own comments in class.

If the teacher does not provide a plan of what is to be covered in the form of handouts or other notes, the student should try to break text up by using headings and sub-headings. It is also a good idea to divide the paper into columns – one for the point being made and another headed, for example, 'implications'. This will really encourage the student to reflect on what is being taught at the time. The "So what?" question is always important. For example:

- "There is variation in the way that students learn"
- "So what?"
- "So, we need to find out how students learn best, and try to accommodate to these different methods."

If the student can't answer the "So what?" question then that is a good sign that he or she needs to clarify understanding with the teacher and the sooner this is done, the better.

How to help – structuring notes

☞ Learners should be encouraged to **develop a structure** that suits the topic and the task. For example, they might want to make notes from a text using the following headings:
- background to the event or topic
- the context – why is the event important?
- who are the main players in the event?
- what is the main part – the key event that can almost sum up the whole topic?
- how does it conclude? Is it an appropriate conclusion? What else could have happened?

☞ The **'helping hand'** technique can help students to structure a response to a topic:

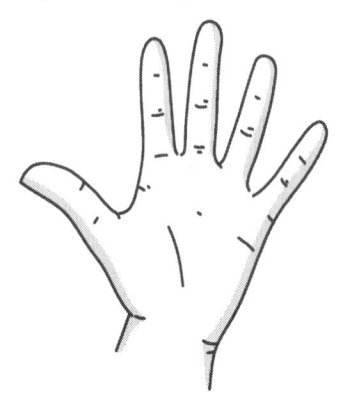

From the thumb to the pinkie, pupils can use their fingers to help elicit a response to a question. The sequence, which they need to remember, is 'who', 'what', 'why', 'where, and when' – with the thumb as the 'who' and the pinkie as the 'when'.

- thumb = who?
- forefinger = what?
- index finger = why?
- ring finger = where?
- pinkie = when?

The palm of the hand can represent a summary of the main points of the topic. The helping hand technique can also be helpful for revision.

Identifying what is important

Once the student has settled on a method for note-taking, or a combination of methods, some tips about what to write might be useful. That is, as a first step the learner has to decide what is important in relation to the content. To do this, it is a good idea for the student to have some background information about the topic. This will make it easier to decide what is relevant or not. There are a number of ways of deciding the relevant content and it might be useful to develop a chart such as that below (with suggested key information underlined):

Table 4: Content chart for note-taking

Topic	Names	Events	Implications
Castles	Caernarvon Castle	The Glyndwr Rising of 1400–1415, when the castle was besieged	Medieval fortress; last major outbreak for Welsh Independence before the incorporation of Wales into England by the Laws in Wales Acts (1535–1542)
	Edinburgh Castle	Robert I (Robert the Bruce) fought a successful War of Independence against the English	As a result, Scotland remained an independent state throughout the late Middle Ages. Edinburgh Castle is one of the most important strongholds in Scotland
Climate Change	Greta Thunberg – Swedish climate activist	August 2018, she spent her days camped out in front of the Swedish Parliament, holding a sign painted in black letters on a white background that read 'Skolstrejk för klimatet' (School Strike for Climate)	Worldwide protest including school-age children and school shutdowns. She has addressed Heads of State at the United Nations, met with the Pope, sparred with the President of the United States and inspired four million people to call for a global climate strike

The above chart can be used as a template for any form of content, in any subject. Using this chart, the student is more able identify the most relevant content and, if necessary, follow up the key points.

Filing notes

It is absolutely crucial that students file their notes as soon as possible after they have been written. If they are in hard copy, they should be filed in order of subject, and date. This means that it would be good practice to note the date and time whenever the notes are taken.

How to help – note-taking

☞ The **example text** below can be used to illustrate some of the strategies we have described:

> William Wilberforce was born on 24 August 1759 in Hull, Yorkshire, England and he died 29 July 1833 in London. He was a British politician and philanthropist who from 1787 was prominent in the struggle to abolish the slave trade and then to abolish slavery itself in British overseas possessions.
>
> He studied at St John's College at the University of Cambridge, where he became a close friend of the future Prime Minister, William Pitt the Younger, and was known as an amiable companion rather than an outstanding student. In 1780 both he and Pitt entered the House of Commons, and he soon began to support parliamentary reform and Roman Catholic political emancipation. He acquired a reputation for radicalism that later embarrassed him, especially during the French Revolution, when he was chosen an honorary citizen of France (September 1792). From 1815 he upheld the Corn Laws (tariffs on imported grain) and repressive measures against working-class agitation.
>
> Wilberforce's abolitionism was derived in part from evangelical Christianity, to which he was converted in 1784–85. His spiritual advisor became John Newton, a former slave trader who had repented and who had been the pastor at Wilberforce's church when he was a child.
>
> In 1787 Wilberforce helped to found a society for the 'reformation of manners' called the Proclamation Society (to suppress the publication of obscenity) and the Society for Effecting the Abolition of the Slave Trade – the latter more commonly called the Anti-Slavery Society. He and his associates – Thomas Clarkson, Granville Sharp, Henry Thornton, Charles Grant, Edward James Eliot, Zachary Macaulay, and James Stephen – were first called the Saints and afterward (from 1797) the Clapham Sect, of which Wilberforce was the acknowledged leader.
>
> (Source https://www.britannica.com/biography/William-Wilberforce)

There is a great deal of information in this text, and it may be difficult to remember it without some form of organisation. To help to organise this information you can utilise the tips below:

- Use a heading – the most obvious one here is 'William Wilberforce' (if you want to make your notes short, you could use the acronym WW after you have written the heading)

- Number the key points in the order they appear
- Re-arrange the list into what you think is the order of importance
- Create sub-headings from the list – for example:
  - WW's background and education
  - WW's friendships and associates
  - The French Revolution
  - WW's occupation
  - The Proclamation Society
  - WW's vocation
  - WW's achievements
  - Relevance today
- Use bulletpoints to organise information within sub-headings
- Put in some detailed information under these areas
- You can use the sub-headings to create a summary:

William Wilberforce was born on 24 August 1759 in Hull, Yorkshire, England and died 23 July 1833 in London. In 1780, both he and his friend Pitt entered the House of Commons, and he soon began to support parliamentary reform and Roman Catholic political emancipation. From 1815, however, he upheld the Corn Laws (tariffs on imported grain) and repressive measures against working-class agitation. In 1787 Wilberforce helped to found the Society for Effecting the Abolition of the Slave Trade – the latter more commonly called the Anti-Slavery Society.

Chapter 17: Linking new information to prior knowledge

Linking new information to prior knowledge is important for effective learning and self-sufficiency in studying. Being able to make connections makes learning more meaningful and useful. It also helps the learner to acquire an understanding of concepts and the specific ideas that underpin the new learning. So, when learners are able to make connections during learning, it is also usually an indicator that they have a good understanding of the information they are learning.

> **Key Point**
>
> When learners are able to make connections during learning, it is usually an indicator that they have a good understanding of the information.

Locating new information in the context of what the learner already knows is also a very useful study skill to develop. Often, concepts that children come across in one area of learning can be useful in another, and some concepts are relevant to all subjects in the curriculum. For example, when looking at a page of print or a book, there is often a key or an index to the contents or the layout. If students understand this when looking at a History book, then they should also appreciate that this strategy can be used in other subjects and reading materials, even if a key is not present. They will realise that they can work out themselves what the key to the page or the book is.

For example, if a question relates to reasons for the popularity of Shakespeare plays in 17th Century England, the student may need to know about the culture at the time. This could include areas such as the poverty, pastimes and living conditions at the time, as well as the politics – the lack of democracy and frustration of the population, leading to the need for social outlets and comedy and cheap entertainment being available to the masses as a form of escapism. This type of information can be gleaned from a number of different subjects, including English and History, and there can be some overlap. It is important, therefore, that the learner is encouraged to make connections.

Schemas

Schema theory suggests that we have a natural tendency to organise information into units, and that these units are connected by a framework (a schema). The schema has a structure that enables us to categorise information. Our brains do this because some level of organisation helps us to make sense of the world. So, if we have developed an idea, or schema, of what a bird is, then when we see a type we have never come across before, we will recognise it as a bird – because we have a schema in our heads that says something like *"a bird is something that can fly, has feathers, two feet and a beak, and lays eggs"*. We can then categorise this new creature we are looking at – we have somewhere to store that new information (even if the thing we are looking at doesn't have all of these characteristics, we could at least categorise it as 'bird-like'. This is more efficient than storing every new bit of information we come across separately – it's like having a special folder for similar things. As mentioned in the previous chapter, when information is filed in some sort of logical system, there is much more chance that we will be able to remember it later (memory is discussed more fully in Chapter 21). So, our natural default is to refer to our schemas (or 'schemata') to help us understand new information.

We can draw on the concept of schemas to help the learning process. For example, if students take some time before learning something new to think about what they already know about a subject, they can get a good idea of where their knowledge gaps are, and therefore what they need or would like to know. They can also see where that new information would fit into their schema, or how their existing knowledge might need to be reviewed or revised.

Key Point
Developing a schema of a topic helps the learner to organise information, and ensures that he or she starts off by referring to existing background knowledge.

Developing a schema of a topic therefore helps the learner to organise and categorise information, and ensures that he or she starts off by referring to existing background knowledge. This very much aids comprehension and recall. We are far more likely to understand and remember information when we work actively to integrate and organise it in this way. This is important in all school subjects, but it is particularly relevant in subjects like History, where background knowledge is essential for an understanding of some historical events (for example the squabbles over succession to the throne during turbulent periods in English history, or the origins of World War 2). Recent research highlights the need for schools to teach more strategies to encourage independent learning skills (Miller and Strachan, 2020).[30]

Even when young children read a story or a passage, they need to relate this to their existing framework of knowledge in order to understand it. So, new information is often embedded in a story that makes everyday sense to the child. Burden (2002) suggests that the cultural and social context of learning is in fact crucial in mediating how a child learns.[31] This suggests that learning involves more than just the presentation of information. It also embraces factors relating to the whole child, and particularly the child's previous cultural and learning experiences.

So, previous experiences and learning can make new learning meaningful, and that means that it is important to establish these before, or while, new learning is being presented. A schema can help the learner:

- attend to the incoming information
- provide a 'scaffolding' that will help with recall (scaffolding is discussed below)
- make inferences from the passage that also aid comprehension and recall
- utilise his or her previous knowledge
- make recall more accessible, because the learner will have a more comprehensive understanding of the area

---

30 Miller J & Strachan S (2020) *Understanding The Experiences Of Autistic And Dyslexic Women In Transitioning Into Tertiary Education: Presentation At Scottish Parliament Cross-Party Group On Dyslexia, 15 Jan 2020.* Available at: http://gtcsnew.gtcs.org.uk/web/FILES/News-resources/Understanding_the_Experiences_of_Autistic_and_Dyslexic_Women_Transitioning_into_Tertiary_Education.pdf [last accessed 16 January 2021]

31 Burden B (2002) *A Cognitive Approach To Dyslexia: Learning Styles And Thinking Skills* in Reid G & Wearmouth J (Eds) *Dyslexia And Literacy: Theory And Practice.* Chichester: John Wiley and Sons.

How to help – using schemas and existing knowledge

☞ **Discuss schemas** – it is useful for students to understand how they categorise and learn information to help with what is currently being taught. This also develops metacognitive awareness (an understanding of how we learn), and skills that can be drawn on in future studies.

☞ **Pre-learning discussion** You can find out what students already know about a topic, task or text in a number of ways, including:

- brainstorming around the title, chapter heading, picture on the front cover
- word association around key words in the title, or an image in the text
- creating a topic mind map or list of bulletpoints; trying to fill in the key areas and then reflecting on what the learner may already know about these areas
- asking students to reflect on how they can connect things they have learned within and across subjects – connecting schemas to each other

This helps children develop thinking and communication skills. It encourages an active form of learning, and can also help the teacher monitor the child's understanding. It can be used both in learning and assessment. For example, the learner can make up a chart such as the one below.

Post-discussion chart

Discussion topic – key points	What I already know	What I have to find out	Where will I obtain the information?

Scaffolding

'Scaffolding' helps learners to progress to a higher level in a task, by providing just the right amount and type of support needed at that time. It's a bit like providing footholds for climbing. If the footholds are too far apart, they are unreachable, and if they are too close together, this will slow down the climber's progress.

Vygotsky (1978) coined the term 'Zone of Proximal Development' (ZPD) and he defined it as *"the distance between the **actual** developmental level as determined by independent problem-solving, and the level of **potential** development as determined through problem-solving under adult guidance, or in collaboration with more capable peers"*.[4] If we continue with the climbing metaphor, the footholds will allow some climbers to attempt rock faces that they have the physical skills for, but which they couldn't attempt at all without support.

Vygotsky believed that providing appropriate assistance can boost the learner's current level to achieve new learning.[4] It is important, however, that this 'boost' is appropriate for the learner and the task. Factors that can provide an effective zone of proximal development include the presence of a more knowledgeable other – this can be a teacher or indeed a peer – and the types of 'scaffolds' that are available. There can be a significant difference, at any stage in learning, between what a learner can achieve unaided, and what that learner can achieve when there is an instructor/teacher present, and interacting with him or her.

Palinscar and Brown (1984) established a programme of 'reciprocal teaching' to assist the learner to gain fuller understanding of teaching materials.[32] This programme shows how interactions between learner and teacher can establish a 'scaffold' to help the learner to connect his/her existing knowledge and experiences with the new learning. Essentially, this is achieved through effective question-and-answer interactions between the teacher and learner, and this should build on the child's response in order to extend his or her thinking.

Expert View

"The essence of creativity is figuring out how to use what you already know in order to go beyond what you already think."

Jerome Bruner

---

32 Palinscar AS & Brown AL (1984) Reciprocal teaching of comprehension-fostering and comprehension-monitoring activities. *Cogn Instr* 1(2): 117–75.

In the classroom, scaffolding can include modeling a skill, providing hints or cues, and adapting the materials or activities (Copple & Bredekamp, 2009).[33] Silver (2011) suggest that scaffolding should involve:[34]

- assessing the student's knowledge and experience for academic content
- relating the content to what the student understands or can do
- breaking a task into small and manageable tasks
- providing opportunities for feedback
- using verbal cues and prompts that are meaningful and appropriate for the task

How to help – scaffolding techniques

There are a number of activities that can be used by parents, carers and teachers to support the learner:

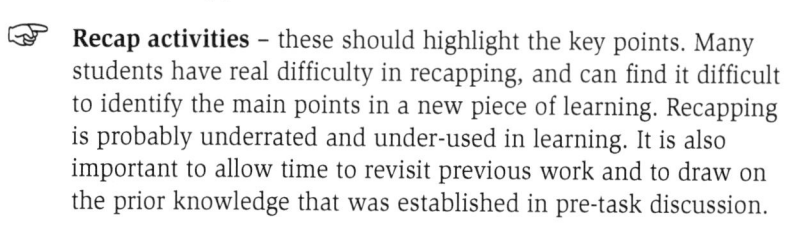

☞ **Recap activities** – these should highlight the key points. Many students have real difficulty in recapping, and can find it difficult to identify the main points in a new piece of learning. Recapping is probably underrated and under-used in learning. It is also important to allow time to revisit previous work and to draw on the prior knowledge that was established in pre-task discussion.

☞ **Bridge-building activities** – one of the most essential aspects of learning is the skill in making connections. Effective learning depends to a great extent on how readily the learner can make connections between the ideas and the content of the material to be learned, and also between the new learning and previous learning. Strategies such as visual imagery, obtaining the main ideas from text, developing concepts through strategies such as mind maps or spider diagrams and self-questioning can all be used to relate previous knowledge with the new material to be learned.

---

33 Copple C & Bredekamp S (2009) *Developmentally Appropriate Practice In Early Childhood Programs Serving Children From Birth Through Age 8*. Washington, DC: National Association for the Education of Young Children.
34 Silver D (2011) Using the 'zone' to help reach every learner. *Kappa Delta Pi Record* 47(1): 28–31.

It is important that students are encouraged to use these strategies. Otherwise, they may become too entrenched in the actual process of reading and notetaking, rather than in the meaning and purpose of the activity. Questions the learner needs to consider are:

- Is there anything about the new learning that is familiar?
- What is familiar, and why?
- How can I use what I know already to help understand and use the new learning?

Asking questions like these will help learners connect between the previous and new learning, and make learning more efficient.

☞ **Using to prevent losing** – it is important that the learner has opportunities to practise the knowledge and skills gained from new learning. It is this practise that leads to automaticity, and it is automaticity that demonstrates that the learner has acquired competence and will be able to use this new skill to help with new learning.

☞ **Consolidation activities** – these are important, and each lesson, or period of learning, needs to finish with a summary of possible consolidation activities. This is essentially overlearning, and is part of the process that can lead to automaticity.

Chapter 18: Problem-solving skills

It is hard to understate how important problem-solving skills are for learning. They help to keep students engaged and enthusiastic, because they encourage a very active approach to learning. That is likely to lead to greater understanding, because 'deep' (rather than 'surface') processing is taking place. Deep processing, in turn, leads to better levels of recall.

> **Key Point**
>
> *When students have developed strategies, and know they can be creative in tackling difficulties, this makes them more confident.*

In addition, problem-solving skills can be useful in tackling exam questions. More generally, when students have developed strategies, and know they can be creative in tackling difficulties, this makes them more confident and more likely to take the kinds of risks that are associated with success in learning and in other areas of life.

Many students are naturally creative in their thinking. This is something that should be valued, and encouraged. It is often seen in 'neurodiverse' students – that is, those who process information differently from most of their peers – and it is particularly important to recognise this positive aspect of learning differences. Some students might need to be supported in uncovering or developing their problem-solving skills.

It is important that children and young people are encouraged to problem-solve from an early age – it is not only for students in secondary school. Even young primary aged children can be encouraged to problem solve, perhaps using pictures, video or other materials. Encouraging younger children to problem-solve will help them further up the school, when they embark on higher level study for exams requiring deeper thinking and problem-solving.

This website has some good suggestions for problem solving in schools and linking this with team building: https://www.theproblemsolvingcompany.co.uk.

How to help – problem-solving skills

☞ **Reassurance** – usually tasks involving problem-solving require a degree of independence and confidence. Some students place a heavy reliance on their teacher to guide them through tasks, and may not have had the practice and developed the confidence to tackle tasks independently, especially open-ended tasks. These students may need some confirmation and reassurance that they are on the right lines and should keep going.

☞ **Develop self-awareness** – this is discussed more fully in Chapter 11. Students need to understand how they learn if they are to become confident, successful and independent. This will encourage them to be more creative, which in turn will improve confidence – it's a 'virtuous circle'!

☞ **Encourage creativity** – create a climate where the student is positively encouraged to try out different approaches, make mistakes, and learn from them. Use 'open-ended' methods such as brainstorming techniques to explore subject areas, problems and exam questions.

☞ **Games and puzzles** – it's a good idea to try to use activities that are fun and also promote problem solving skills. These might include crossword puzzles, 'whodunit?' murder mystery activities, treasure hunts or outdoor field trips looking at landscape or historical artefacts. Problems such as "why is the landscape like this?" or "why was the ruin built in that way" can promote a great deal of problem-solving and deeper thinking. This website has some good ideas: https://teambuilding.com/blog/problem-solving-games.

☞ **Thinking skills programmes** – these can be a useful way of developing self-knowledge and problem-solving skills. The Cort 'Thinking Skills' programme (http://www.cortthinking.com/CoRT) helps learners to develop their breadth of thinking, as well as how they organise their thinking and problem-solving. It can encourage more productive and more efficient thinking. The programme can also help learners to develop the skill of evaluation. As indicated earlier in this chapter, positive feelings are very important for successful learning and this is also considered in this thinking programme.

Edward de Bono's work is also useful. For example, his book *Six Thinking Hats* (1995) is an excellent resource for developing thinking through the analogy of 'thinking hats'.[35] The technique aims to allow students to separate emotion from logic and creativity from information. Essentially, de Bono defines and describes the nature and contribution of different types of thinking. Colours are used to describe different types of thinking. For example, 'white hat thinking' relates to facts and figures, 'red hat thinking' to emotions and feelings, 'black hat thinking' to negative assessment, 'yellow hat thinking' to speculative and positive thinking, 'green hat thinking' to creative and lateral thinking, and 'blue hat thinking' to focusing and controlling thinking.

This website has some good ideas on thinking skills: https://www.brighthorizons.com/family-resources/developing-critical-thinking-skills-in-children.

☞ **Discussion** – this is an ideal way to enhance learning and help students move from surface to deep learning. Discussion can help them reframe their ideas and think about points in the topic they have not considered. It is useful to prepare a framework for discussion rather than leave it open-ended. You can provide a controversial question than can provoke a discussion, perhaps a heated one - and that is good as it shows the students are becoming involved in the topic. You can also list a number of questions on the topic and it is a good idea to include simple as well as thought-provoking ones. These can include the following types of questions:

- **Literal questions:** that is merely re-interpreting in their own words what the text is indicating. Try to discourage pure copying but obviously students may use some of the words that are in the text, particularly the key words.
- **Inferential questions:** this is moving to deeper thinking and asking questions that may not be obvious from the text. This goes beyond the basic information in the text.
- **Deductive questions:** to deduce is also a high level skill and this can be practiced using pictures – e.g. showing the students a picture such as a calamitous scene and asking them to draw conclusions. You can then move on to basic text and then more complex narrative.

---

35 De Bono E (1995) *Edward de Bono's Mind Power*. London: Dorling Kindersley.

- **Justification:** this is when the students have to find evidence for a particular viewpoint. This is also a deep level skill and they have to ensure that the point they are making can be supported by the evidence.
- **Statement prompts:** this is probably the easiest way to encourage discussion. Statements can be provided and the students have to say whether they are or disagree with them.

Chapter 19: Understanding what is being taught

Wray (1994) suggests that the difference between good and poor readers is that poor readers take a passive role.[36] They lack a clear purpose of reading, view reading as essentially a decoding task, and seldom re-read or actively comprehend while they read. Good readers, however, take an active role in the learning process.

Expert View

"One of the things which distinguishes effective readers is the ability to take decisions about which reading strategy to adopt, and when to switch."

David Wray

This principle applies more generally for learning that might be achieved through a variety of means (that is, not just by reading). As we have stressed in this book, it is important to encourage learners to develop confidence and independence, so we need to explore ways of helping them to understand what is being taught, while developing metacognitive awareness and generic skills that they can draw on for their future learning.

There is no quick fix for studying and learning – effective learning starts with effective teaching. Learning is best carried out at the point of teaching, and not six months down the road during a period of 'revision'. One of the most important factors is understanding. If the learner understands the information or new learning, then there is a greater chance it will be retained and recalled when necessary. Additionally, the learner will be able to take the next step and look at the inferences relating to the new learning – for example *Why is it important? What are the implications of the new learning?* By reflecting in this way, learners will be better able to respond when asked about the subject in class, and to deal with the trickier questions that can appear in exam papers (essay-writing and exams are discussed more fully in Chapters 23-26).

This is also important for younger learners, including those in the early stages of primary/elementary school. It is important that they are able to manipulate new learning and recognise the implications of this – they need to be taught to ask the 'why?' questions. Once learners do this, they

---

36 Wray D (1994) *Literacy And Awareness*. London: Hodder & Stoughton.

have become active learners – and it is well-established that learning is more successful when it is active rather than passive.

Exploratory and investigative learning is crucial for learners of all ages. Fortunately, we have access to a mountain of information through the Internet, and this can provide learners with the information they need along with the opportunity to ask those crucial questions that can help learning become more personal, relevant and effective.

How to help – understanding what is being taught

☞ **Self-questioning** – the student needs to ask him- or herself what the key points are, and why these are important. It can even be useful to question why this topic is being taught – what its place is in the subject (e.g. History, Geography, etc.) and what its importance is in that subject. This helps the learner to feel a sense of ownership, and to gain the confidence to 'question the question'. This in turn leads to a higher degree of understanding and it certainly promotes enquiry skills, which are also essential for full comprehension of a topic area.

☞ **Discussion of concepts** – if a learner has good conceptual understanding, then he or she will have a good understanding of the features of a topic or individual aspects of the topic. For example, if a learner has a good conceptual understanding of the theme of 'pollution' this would mean he or she also has an understanding of the different facets that make up an understanding of the environment and climate change.

☞ **Key words** – it is important to help children identify key words and key points in a text. These can help with understanding, but they can also act as a trigger point for study and recall in an exam. Once the key words or points are identified, children can obtain some further help in organising them into categories, ideas and themes. This can help to build concepts and ideas, as well as helping with memory.

☞ **Use headings** – when reading for facts, the student can make a checklist of different types of information under different headings. It may also be helpful if the teacher actually provides the headings for the student, at least until this skill has been consolidated.

☞ **Association** – encourage children to place together words, or pieces of text that have a common link. This helps with understanding and it encourages an active role in reading. It will also help them to remember more information and to be able to recall it in a more organised and structured manner. For example, if they are recalling information about a famous battle, all the facts about uniforms, weapons, locations and the countries involved can be linked together. For older children, the leaders of the different countries and their policies can also be added to this. Using associations is good practice for making connections, and this can help develop thinking and learning skills.

☞ **Summarising** – it is our view that if a learner can summarise the information, then it is well-learned and understood. It is good for students to practise summarising and they do not have to be too ambitious at the start. Ask pupils to:

- first, underline what you consider to be the key words
- write sentences or phrases with each of those key words
- put the sentences in order
- try to combine several sentences, and try to shorten them by omitting some words that may not be necessary.

☞ **Evaluating** – this involves making judgements, and it is a good idea to help the learner (even from a very young age) to make judgements and provide opinions on what he or she is reading. Ask questions like "Which do you think is best, and why?", "Do you think ___ made the correct choice?" and "Why do you think this?". This type of exercise is good practice, and helps with comprehension and thinking skills. If the learner understands the materials/text and is able to make *judgements* on this, then studying does not become a memory chore, but a learning experience.

☞ **Listening** – listening skills can help to develop attention, help to equip children to become more aware of others, and in turn to become better learners. It is important that listening is given a high priority but it is equally important that listening should be interspersed with other forms of learning, particularly discussion.

☞ **Taking a 'brain break'** – Carey (2015) suggests that deliberate interruption, particularly when engaged in a big project such as a long essay or dissertation, can be helpful.[19] That is, the learner should take time out to focus elsewhere and he or she will then begin to see other things in daily life that are relevant. These can

begin to see other things in daily life that are relevant. These can provide clues for a way forward. This seems similar to something we have all experienced – when we stop actively trying to remember something, the brain will at some later stage come up with the answer! Carey calls this the 'percolation process', and it is one that can help with clarification in a task that is complex.[19]

☞ **Role-play** – one of the key points about developing learning skills is that learning should be personalised by the learner. This will make learning more meaningful, and will help to develop comprehension skills. One way of achieving this is to develop imagination. Role-play can be an excellent tool for this. It helps to facilitate children's creativity and furthermore can make learning individual.

☞ **Drama** – many children will develop comprehension more effectively if they are actively involved in a participatory activity. Both role play and drama use the kinaesthetic modality, and this experiential type of learning can be invaluable for many learners. Not only can it instil confidence and boost self-esteem; it can also make information more meaningful, and help to develop social and language skills.

☞ **Collaborating** – learning can be more enjoyable and more effective if there are opportunities for collaboration. Group work is important, but it is also important to ensure that the group dynamics are positive for all the learners. Some children may feel intimidated in a group, whereas others can feel bored. It is important that signs anxiety or boredom in the group are noted and acted upon.

☞ **Feedback** – this is an important aspect of learning, as it can reinforce the learning process. Positive feedback can help to develop confidence and help the learner take risks with future learning. This helps the learner to extend his or her creativity, and can provide more independence in learning.

☞ **Feelings** – it is important to recognise that learning involves the whole person, and that the emotional aspects of learning matter. It is important to establish any anxieties the child may be experiencing around the learning process and to deal with these in an appropriate way. Some children may only need an opportunity to speak to an adult, whereas others may need ongoing support.

Comprehension

Wray (1994) notes that good readers take an active role – that is, they generate questions while they read, and also transfer what they read into mental images, and will re-read if necessary, so that they actively comprehend while they read.[36] These strategies should be discussed with pupils, so that they are aware of how useful they are in understanding and learning. We look at active processing of information in more detail in Chapter 22.

Reciprocal teaching was mentioned in Chapter 17. It is integral to helping the learner to develop thinking and learning skills that can be used when studying independently. Reciprocal teaching both monitors and enhances comprehension by focusing on processes relating to questioning, clarifying, summarising and predicting (Palinscar & Brown, 1984).[32] The teacher leads the discussion by asking questions. This generates additional questions from participants, and the questions are then clarified by the teacher and participants together. The discussion is then summarised by the teacher or participants. Following this, a new 'teacher' is selected by the participants to lead the discussion on the next section of the text. Using this procedure, learners can become teachers. Teaching is one of the best ways to ensure you know the material!

How to help – encouraging comprehension

☞ Below are some prompts that can be used to develop understanding and to help learners gain some knowledge of the type of questions to ask when they are working independently:

- What do you think about…?
- What makes you think that?
- What words give you that impression?
- How do you feel about…?
- Can you explain why…?
- Do you agree with ___'s opinion?
- Do you like the bit where…?
- I wonder if…
- Is there anything that puzzles you?

- I'm not sure what I think about… I wonder what the writer intended…
- This bit reminds me of…
- I would hate to have that happen to me – would you?
- I like the way the writer has…
- Are there any patterns you notice (e.g. familiar story structure, images)?
- I wonder why the writer has decided to…

Visual learning

Many learners might find they can understand material more easily if it is in a visual format, or they are able to convert it into that type of format. Some students may need to be trained to use visual skills, whereas others can use this method quite instinctively. Many apps for study are very visual, and these can be helpful, but there is no reason why the learner cannot convert his or her own materials to a visual format for ease of understanding and recall. Imaginative and visual skills can involve students developing ideas from visualising, or imagining details that may be inferred but not explicitly shown. For example, in a story they may be asked the following:

- What might the weather have been like?
- Where do you think the story took place?
- Describe the scene
- What were the main colours?
- Describe the main characters

These questions can help to encourage students to think of the topic visually. This strategy can be applied to all topics. For example, to take a scene from a historical battle, the students can look at a picture of the battle and from that they can address the above questions. This can help to bring the topic to life, and this also enhance understanding and recall. Children can be encouraged to draw, but it is important for them to know that it doesn't matter if they can't (or feel they can't) draw. Pupils can practise developing their visual skills through activities. One such activity (from Reid, Guise and Guise [2018]) is shown below:[37]

---

[37] Reid G, Guise N & Guise J (2018) *The Big Book Of Dyslexia: Practical Activities For Kids And Teens*. London: Jessica Kingsley Publishers.

How to help – visual learning activity

☞ For this activity you will need a collection of pictures or images. From these, choose ten to place on the wall for display. You should number these. The images can be art pictures, media photos or magazine portrayals. Old calendars are a great source for images and this can also help with recycling out-of-date calendars.

☞ Select a picture and discuss any characters, objects, colours, scenes and the general content with the students. You can then introduce the word 'annotation' and discuss this term with them. Demonstrate this process a number of times.

☞ You then ask students to make notes about the image you selected while you are discussing it with them.

☞ After this warm-up, give the students a picture number each to study. Ideally, these should be on the wall behind them, or in some other suitable location (so that they are not visible to the students after they have studied them).

☞ Set a timer for three minutes and, when it sounds, the students return to their seat. Ensure the images they studied are no longer in sight. The students should then list as many things as they can remember about their picture.

☞ Offer students an option to sketch the image from memory, if this is easier for them. Allow five to ten minutes for this part of the activity. On completion of this stage, they can return to the images, and check how well they did!

☞ You can now ask them to describe their pictures while looking at the image. Discuss with them how this helps. A further option is to carry out this activity in pairs and see if this helps them with recall. They can consider the benefits of teamwork and combining their strengths.

Chapter 20: Making subject teaching learner-friendly

In secondary/high school, learning is usually organised by subjects or themes. Although most of the subject content is determined by examination considerations and prescribed curricula, much can still be done to identify the potential areas of the curriculum that may present difficulties for some students. There is no reason, therefore, why the content of all subjects cannot be developed in a learner-friendly manner.

It is important that all teachers have insights into how children learn, as well as the content of the subject they are teaching. It can be argued that the principles for making information learner-friendly are the same for every subject. The key to achieving this, along with an awareness of how children learn, is forward planning. This also implies skills in curriculum differentiation, an understanding of learning styles and learner-friendly strategies.

Key Point
There is no reason why the content of all subjects cannot be developed in a learner-friendly manner.

In this chapter we will present examples of learner-friendly approaches to teaching across different subject areas of the curriculum.

English
In English, it is important to use a range of sources and make learning as experiential as possible. It is often best to begin with discussion, so that the overall story and plot can be understood by all before any reading and investigation takes place. This can help to build concepts and a 'schema' of the topic. The 'schema' essentially refers to the student's own understanding of a situation or an event. More information on schemas can be found in Chapter 17. It is important that the student has an appropriate schema before commencing to read. This will help with subsequent understanding and will be very important when the student is studying for exams.

Geography
Geography can be very accessible, experiential and practical. It has the potential to be highly visual and the subject content relates to the study of people and activities in the community and world around us.

In other words, it is a subject that has direct relevance to living in today's world. This means that information in Geography can be accessed in a variety of ways – visually, in field trips and visits, and in interviews and observation, quite apart from using reading materials. It is important that students are able to take notes during field trips and visits, and to compile their own logs as they progress with the trips. It is also important that they record the purpose of the trip, and what they achieved from it.

Geography can involve visual-spatial abilities. Visual-spatial ability (also described as 'visuo-spatial ability') is the capacity to understand, reason and remember the spatial relations between objects or within a space. Visual-spatial abilities have everyday use in navigation, understanding or fixing equipment, understanding or estimating distance and measurement, and practical performance on a job. Practice in developing visual-spatial skills can be useful in Geography, and it can also have benefits for a range of other curricular areas. Many different activities can help with visual-spatial abilities, and one is shown below.

How to help – 'North, South, East, West'

☞ Take a map of the world – a wall map or a globe would both work. In groups, children should make up questions for another group on the location of some countries in relation to other countries. They can use the compass points between the main points, e.g. North, North-West. A globe might be more challenging and this can be good for older students (adapted from Reid, Reid & Guise, 2018).[37]

Additionally, Geography by its very nature incorporates an 'enquiry approach' in developing subject knowledge and understanding. This can be seen in the following statement: *"Geography develops knowledge of places and environments throughout the world, an understanding of maps, and a range of investigative and problem-solving skills, both inside and outside the classroom. As such it prepares pupils for adult life and employment"* (DfEE and QCA, 1999).[38] It is important that Geography – and, in fact, every subject – is underpinned by understanding. This can help with retention and also gain learner confidence.

---

38   DfEE (Department for Employment and Education) and QCA (Qualifications and Curriculum Authority (1999) *The National Curriculum For England: Geography*. London: DfEE and QCA.

History

History is a subject that can be stimulating and engaging for students if it is taught in an investigative and real-life manner. History demands investigation and skills in problem-solving.

Dargie (2001) suggests that discussion holds the key to this.[39] Talking about an issue, he suggests, can help pupils rehearse the separate components of a topic and develop an argument that they can then use in written work. Dargie also suggests that students can gain experience in the range of specific skills needed for History, such as the ability to question, infer, deduce, propose, estimate, guess, judge and to think.

Learning to talk about History can provide a launch pad for reading and writing about History. Similarly, paired homework, with an emphasis on pupils having to check that their partner can readily explain topic vocabulary, can also provide the confidence to write.

Many excellent audio and visual resources exist for most History courses. YouTube videos can bring the subject to life in an exciting and lively manner, and in doing so clarify concepts and events for all learners.

How to help – creating self-aware readers

☞ It is important to plan a reading strategy that seeks to create more 'self-aware' readers who understand the purpose of their reading, and who appreciate how and why the text in front of them is shaped in the way that it is. Taking History as our example, an effective reading strategy might include features such as:

- consistent teacher pre-checking of text material and calculation of reading age to ensure that pupils encounter historical text in a planned, progressive way
- a focus on concept vocabulary and on discursive connectives that develop historical argument

---

39 Dargie R (2001) *Dyslexia And History* in Peer L & Reid G (Eds) *Dyslexia: Successful Inclusion In The Secondary School.* London: David Fulton.

- the selective use of word-processing functions such as emboldening and/or increasing point size to highlight the way historical text works
- the planned reading of material as homework, to increase pupil familiarity with the demands of the text, using scissors and highlighter pens to analyse how different kinds of historical text are constructed
- highlighting photocopied text according to given criteria – for example, from a search of key phrases
- persistent teacher questioning to accompany pupil reading to check comprehension
- teacher awareness of the different preferred reading styles of pupils, and of the interactive nature of effective reading
- teacher awareness of the difficulties posed by 'weasel words' in History (e.g. class, state, party, church) that have an abstract historical usage in addition to their more familiar, common concrete meaning
- teacher awareness of the need to structure their own writing to meet the needs of different learners – for example, by:
    - avoiding long, multiclausal sentences
    - avoiding the over-use of passive voice constructions
    - planning ways of explaining unfamiliar vocabulary and ideas, e.g. by using 'word boxes' (see example below)

New Vocabulary	Meaning

- 'marginal scaffolding' (providing just enough support to the learner to enable him or her to carry out the task)
- keeping text concrete rather than abstract, where appropriate
- minimising the use of metaphorical language
- being alert to the range of tenses used in history to describe actions in the past (adapted from Dargie, 2001).[39]

Physics
Physics is a subject that can present some difficulties to many students, but it is also one of the subjects in which gifted learners in particular can do very well, because it may involve a high degree of scientific understanding. In Physics, it is important to draw connections with other subjects, as this will help with understanding.

Drama
Drama is a subject that should be enjoyable and easily accessed by students. Drama utilises a wide range of practical and experiential skills that can include planning the sets and designing costumes. Students can work in pairs through the various scenes in a play, completing columns with lists of props, character costumes and ideas for scenery.

One of the important aspects about drama is that it has cross-curricular implications. It can have a positive spin-off effect in English, Art and other subjects. Subjects such as Drama have the opportunity to boost a student's self-concept and this can have a transferable effect to other subject areas.

Social sciences
One of the key aspects about social science subjects is that there is usually a considerable amount of writing associated with them. History in particular can have a lot of both reading and writing. It is important to try to make this as learner-friendly as possible. Some strategies for social sciences subjects are shown below.

How to help – making social sciences learner-friendly

☞ **Writing** – writing frames can be useful, because they provide a structure to help students follow both the sequence of what they are writing and to extend the content. To help to extend writing, and it is a good idea to provide students with around six pictures and ask them to make comments on each. The comments could then form the main points of the written work.

☞ **Sequencing information** – this can be problematic for some learners, and it may place demands on working memory. It might be a good idea to use paper with numbered squares or to use a timeline.

☞ **Discussion** – as noted previously in this book, discussion helps children gather their thoughts. It is helpful to make it personal and concrete, for example by encouraging children to bring in photos or objects, which can be the basis for their contribution to the discussion.

☞ **Categorising information** – this is a skill that often needs to be learned. It is very important for organisation, and this helps with clarity when studying independently. There can often be a great deal of information in subjects like History, and organising the information can be a real challenge for some learners. It can be helpful to present information in chunks, with some description attached to the information. This helps the learner to categorise the information, which in turn helps with both understanding and recall. It also helps with schema development, which is necessary to develop concepts and higher-order thinking skills.

☞ **Investigation** – this is quite a major part of many subjects in school, and certainly in social science subjects. It is a good idea to provide children with a work plan indicating the procedure and the resources that are necessary for an investigation. They need to have the steps clearly laid out, almost in the form of a checklist.

☞ **Memory** – social science subjects can have a heavy content, with a lot of information to remember. This can place some strain on memory. Strategies for memory are highlighted in a number of chapters in this book, but the important point that can be reiterated here is that these strategies should be personalised for the individual student. What can be provided is some guidance on how to develop a more effective memory using the student's own strategies.

Music and Art

Both Music and Art are subjects that some students can do well in by utilising creativity and artistic skills. Both subject also require a degree of reading accuracy. This can provide a barrier for some, even if they have skills in Music and Art. It is important that any literacy barriers do not prevent students from reaching their potential in these areas.

How to help – challenges and strategies in Music and Art

☞ Challenges and strategies in Music

Challenges	Strategies
The reading of music scores can be like learning a new language. Students have to learn the meaning of symbols, some with only subtle differences between them, and know when and how to use these symbols	Use colour as much as possible to distinguish between the different types of notes
Visual processing – convergence difficulties tracking difficulties	Use coloured paper, coloured overlays Enlarge a normal-sized score
Speed of processing difficulties	Present the music score in short pieces
Co-ordination difficulties	Allow the student to master the instrument first before reading the music
Frustration	Emphasise that there is no competition – set small, achievable targets

☞ Challenges and strategies in Art

Challenge	Strategies
Visual processing – inability to see the detail of a painting	Use viewfinders to narrow down the perspective on a chosen painting.
Remembering the styles of different artists	Use themes such as line and movement (Van Gogh), hues and shades (Monet), pattern and shape (Klimt), distortion and bold use of colour (Picasso)
Understanding the artist's motives and feelings	Visits to galleries looking at the biographical details of the artists are helpful. Use audio aids at galleries to obtain this information. Back in class, bring these up in circle time to further explore the artist's feelings and mood

Challenges and strategies in Art (continued)

Challenge	Strategies
Visual processing – inability to see the detail of a painting	Use viewfinders to narrow down the perspective on a chosen painting.
Remembering the styles of different artists	Use themes such as line and movement (Van Gogh), hues and shades (Monet), pattern and shape (Klimt), distortion and bold use of colour (Picasso)
Understanding the artist's motives and feelings	Visits to galleries looking at the biographical details of the artists are helpful. Use audio aids at galleries to obtain this information. Back in class, bring these up in circle time to further explore the artist's feelings and mood
Misconceptions of Art as a school subject – many feel it is not academic, and only practical	Investigate famous artists and how they influenced society – see 'Ten Paintings that Changed the World': https://www.voicemag.uk/feature/885/ten-paintings-that-changed-the-world
Following sequential instructions – many of the instructions in Art and Design follow a sequence that is necessary for the product to be completed properly	Present the instructions one at a time. Ensure one stage is successfully completed before the student moves on to the next stage
Technical vocabulary – many new and unfamiliar words will be used in art and design technology; this can be demanding for some students	Ask the student to develop a personalised dictionary. This should include the technical words with the meaning and, if possible, an illustration
Complex diagrams and instructions – even pictorial instructions can be complex	Ensure that each component of the diagram is annotated. This will help the student identify the pieces, and see where the different components fit into the whole

Languages

Modern Foreign Languages (MFL) can prove challenging for some students, but they can lend themselves quite easily to kinaesthetic approaches by focusing on experiential learning activities, which are helpful for many students. Examples are shown below (adapted from Crombie and McColl, 2001):[40]

- using charts and diagrams to highlight the 'bigger picture'
- adding pictures to text
- using colour to highlight grammatical features such as gender, accents
- labelling diagrams and charts
- using games to consolidate vocabulary
- making packs of pocket-sized revision cards
- using different colours for different purposes
- using mind maps and/or spider diagrams
- allowing students to produce their own audio recordings
- providing an interest in the country, through showing films, and highlighting literature and culture

Implications for other subjects

The examples above highlight how different subject areas can be accessed and understood, helping the student become a more competent learner. They also illustrate that the suggestions, and the principles upon which these suggestions are based, can be applied across the whole curriculum. All subjects, including the sciences, social sciences and subjects of a more practical and technical orientation, can be made learner-friendly. The key principles include planning as well as an awareness of the difficulties and the strengths shown by the students in the class.

It is also important to recognise the role of learning styles, and the need to present information in a manner and mode that is consistent with each student's learning style. One cannot underestimate the potential of cross-curricular learning and the importance of this for all students.

---

40 Crombie M & McColl H (2001) *Dyslexia And The Teaching Of Modern Foreign Languages* in Peer L & Reid G (Eds) *Dyslexia And Inclusion In The Secondary School*. London: David Fulton Publishers.

Chapter 21: Supporting and improving memory

Throughout this book, we have shown that there are many factors that can have an impact on how well students will remember what they have learned. The personal and interpersonal environment are important and, if information is understood well at the point of learning and linked to former knowledge, students are much more likely to retain it.

Key Point

Any activity that involves multi-tasking will have a working memory element, and it is easy to see the impact this could have on learning.

It can also be useful for students to have access to some specific strategies to boost memory and, in particular, we need to consider the different roles of working memory and long-term memory. 'Working memory' is used to describe our capacity to hold information while manipulating or working on it. For example, you would be using working memory if you were carrying out mental arithmetic, or trying to retain verbal instructions while carrying out a task. Long-term memory, by contrast, is where we store learned information that we want to keep indefinitely.

Working memory is also used when we are taking notes. If we are taking notes from a written source (a book, a whiteboard or blackboard), we have to look at the text, remember what we can, write it down, then go back to the text and continue. Clearly, the more we can remember in one pass, the quicker we will be in writing notes. The student who has difficulties in working memory might find that he or she runs out of time, and that the board has been wiped or deleted or the teacher has moved on. Difficulties with working memory are even more apparent when the student has to take notes while the teacher is talking. In fact, any activity that involves multi-tasking will have a working memory element, and it is easy to see the impact this could have on learning.

The following are quotes from pupils and parents of pupils who were assessed with working memory difficulties:

"It's hard. You don't want to admit it. You bottle it up, because people make fun of you every day." (D, aged 14)

"He would have massive tantrums at home – frustration, anger, tears. Homework was such a challenge. It was hard for me, or anyone else, to understand." (D's mother)

"I feel very awkward, like, what was I going to say? I keep thinking about it. I get very nervous in talks and get sore tummies. It's embarrassing." (E, aged 9)

The key characteristic of working memory is that when information is forgotten, it is gone forever. This is sometimes referred to a 'catastrophic loss'. Furthermore, students don't always know that they have forgotten something (for instance, part of an instruction) – because they have forgotten it! So, they might finish a task thinking they had done exactly what was asked, and then be very disappointed (and puzzled) to discover subsequently that they did badly. This can affect students' confidence and morale. Therefore, it's extremely important to ascertain if there might be some difficulties in working memory.

Working memory is thought to be separate from long-term memory, and this means that a student who has difficulties with working memory could nevertheless be good at learning and retaining information. However, working memory difficulties might affect the student's access to long-term memory stores – it may take longer to consolidate information in long-term memory, and there can be delays in retrieving it. These delays are sometimes referred to as 'word-finding difficulties'.

In Chapter 17, we discussed schema theory – i.e. we tend to categorise knowledge, and if we link new information to existing schemas we will understand and remember it better. It is also useful to consider other characteristics of long-term memory that make recall easier. In particular, we remember things well if they form a story or a narrative (and especially if the story is unusual or exciting, and if it forms part of our personal experience). In addition, if we forget part of a story, we can often figure out the missing information from what we do know.

Identifying problems with memory is absolutely crucial, because usually memory problems are not obvious to the teacher, parent or carer, or the pupil. A child cannot be expected to know how well his or her memory works compared to others in the class. From the teacher, parent or carer's point of view, it might seem that the child is not listening, not motivated, or 'easily distracted'. If working memory is poor, the child might well be easily distracted (so this could be seen as effect, rather than cause), and might look for other ways of keeping focused and on-task.

How to help – identifying memory problems

☞ **Key characteristics** of a child having a difficulty with working memory are:

- doesn't take notes (for the reasons described above of being unable to retain sufficient information in one pass)
- vocalises or chats while working; this can be a strategy developed by the pupil to stay 'on-task'
- interrupts - because he or she has to say what is on his or her mind before the information is forgotten
- avoids or complains about work that involves concentration, because he or she finds this extremely challenging
- can't get started on a task, because competing thoughts about what to do cause confusion and this can lead to inaction
- forgets instructions for a task, abandons task before it is complete, or gets lost in the task

☞ **Other clues** can be seen in the pupil's behaviour:

- inattentive/zoning out
- appears tired (it can be exhausting to keep focused and to keep concentrating)
- appears anxious – if the child has a sense that he or she is never going to remember what was said, or what needs to be done, this can be quite stressful
- fidgets, rocks in chair, clicks pen – these activities can distract others, but they may be what is keeping the pupil's attention 'in the room'
- impulsive – e.g. answering quickly before information is lost
- writing on hand
- using fingers to count
- reserved in large group settings – it can be hard to keep up with conversations that involve a lot of people
- over-use of highlighter – when asked to mark key words, the pupil marks every word, to help keep focus on the text
- forgetful… would you send this pupil on an errand?
- difficulties in following every step of instructions

- place-keeping difficulties – forgetting where he or she was in a piece of text
- problems in retaining and processing information
- incomplete recall
- problems with planning and organising
- tendency in essays to drift off-topic
- failure to complete work in allocated time
- difficulty with mental maths, learning times tables and remembering formulae
- inconsistent pupil performance, e.g.:
  - understands number concepts, but gets sums wrong
  - good results in spelling tests, but 'silly' mistakes in written work
  - good word reading, but difficulties in comprehension

Strategies for learners with working memory difficulties

If a child has been having to work at a more intense level, or if he or she is putting in the same effort as others in the class, then he or she is probably not getting the success that would be expected (or the positive reinforcement that would come with this). For this reason, it is important to remove the burden from working memory as much as possible when working with young people facing challenges of this kind.

The following strategies have been shown to be useful in classroom situations (and can be adapted for tasks done at home):

- Promote self-efficacy
- Use multisensory techniques
- Simplify linguistic structures
- Restructure large task into separate steps
- Reduce processing demands
- Provide external memory aids

These will be discussed in more detail below.

Promote self-efficacy and confidence

The following tactics can be used to improve students' feelings of self-efficacy and confidence:

- overlearning – revising and reviewing information until it is fully consolidated
- encouraging pupils to ask for help
- self-testing and self-questioning
- metacognitive training
- using known strengths and learning styles
- relaxation

It can be helpful to bear in mind, and tell our students, that our brains aren't designed to remember everything – if we did, we would be overloaded with information. Carey (2015) suggests that it is normal to forget and that this actually shows the brain is working.[19] He describes the 'theory of dis-use', which suggests that the brain is working efficiently by discarding information that is not necessary. So, what learners need to do is find out how their memories work, and how to make the best use of the memory that they have.

Use multisensory techniques

There are different types of long-term memory, including narrative (taking the form of a story), autobiographical and episodic (relating to a specific event in the person's life). These memories tend to have some coherence, and structure – they can be seen as stories that have a beginning, a middle and an end, and that is what makes them easier to remember. So, we could encourage learners to create stories, or establish similar patterns to help them to remember information.

For example, it can be useful for the student to develop rituals or habits in studying and learning. If he or she has a tendency to forget or lose track of notes, then colour-coding might be useful – all English notes in a green folder, Biology notes in a blue folder and so on. Then, when it comes to moments such as checking the right folder is in the bag or choosing where to file handouts, the answer should be obvious. It's best if students decide for themselves what colour-coding works best for them. We can extend this principle to the use of templates, or flow charts, to complete schoolwork, such as essays or maths formulae. The benefit of this is that after some practice, the method chosen becomes automatic, and this means that there is no burden on working memory.

If students are learning about an author, or a period of history, it is likely that he or she will find it easier to remember if there is some autobiographical or episodic memory that can be used as a link. This could be visiting a museum, a site of historic interest or an author's birthplace, or seeing the author at a book-reading. Part of the appeal of this type of learning is that it is multisensory. The more senses that are used, the more interesting is the experience, and the more ways there are of tracing that memory. Some pupils will find that they are more likely to remember things they have heard, and they will find it helpful to use auditory methods – reading aloud, or listening to a recording. Visual learners will find it easier to remember information that is in the form of mind maps or pictures. Most learners will find it useful, even if they have a particular preference, to vary the types of input.

Simplify linguistic structures

When giving instructions, setting maths questions, or looking at text comprehension, it is important to look at sentence construction, because sometimes the pupil is not able to carry out the task because of the way it has been presented. It helps if sentence makes sense as it unfolds, so consider word order and the use of the passive voice. For example, "the boy that was carried by the girl had red hair" is much harder to understand on first reading than "the girl carried the red-haired boy." Similarly, in the Maths problem "after Jill has eaten three of his sweets, John has only five left. How many did John have to start with?", it is quite difficult to know what arithmetic is required. The same task could be presented in a more accessible way: "How many sweets did John have to start with? Jill ate three, and he has five left."

Restructure large tasks into separate steps

The hardest type of task for a learner who has difficulties with memory is one that is large and unstructured. It can also seem quite daunting and discouraging. So, it is very helpful to break tasks down into manageable steps. This way, the student only has to think of one or two things at a time, and can progress through a big task step-by-step. He or she will have a feeling of progress, and is more likely to succeed, which itself can lead to greater achievement. Breaking tasks into separate steps can be done in different ways, depending on the topic. The following are useful strategies:

- create checklists or flow charts
- use close reading strategies – read the first sentence of every paragraph, look for key words, then read each paragraph and take notes section by section
- break down maths calculations into stages that could be colour-coded
- use a template or structure for writing – for example, introduction, argument (providing a short number of key points), conclusion

Reduce processing demands

As noted above, note-taking can be challenging and if this is the case, it should be minimised. Note-taking is discussed in more detail in Chapter 16. It can help to provide students with key points and/or specific vocabulary they will need to carry out a task. The aim – as always – would be to encourage them to develop the skills to do this for themselves as they progress in their learning.

There is a wide range of Information Technology (IT) that can be used to help with reading, writing and organising information, and the following are popular:

- Clicker software (https://www.cricksoft.com/uk/clicker)
- CoWriter (https://cowriter.com)
- Notability (https://www.gingerlabs.com/)
- Read&Write Texthelp (https://www.gingerlabs.com/)
- Dragon Naturally Speaking (https://www.nuance.com/en-gb/dragon.html)

More apps and programs can be found in Table 5 below.

Table 5: Assistive technology

Text to speech (TTS)
Claro Read – Claro software
Read and Write – TextHelp
Sprint Plus – Jabbla
Read aloud (right mouse button Microsoft Edge browser)
Immersive reader – Office 365 online
Select a Speech – iOS (settings > Accessibility)
C Pen Reader (Hardware)
C Pen exam Reader (Hardware)

Speech to Text
Dragon Professional Individual – Nuance
Dictate – Office 365 online
Dictate – Word Desktop – Office 365
Dictation – Windows 10 (Windows Key + H)
Dictation – iOS
Dictation- MacOS (Function Key three time)

Note-taking
Audio Notetaker – Sonocent
Livescribe (Hardware)
Olympus DM-770 Digital Voice Recorder (Hardware)
OneNote – Microsoft
Evernote – evernote.com

Access to mind-mapping software, such as Inspiration and iMindMap could also be useful to help with expression of ideas, structuring and planning projects and work, for organisational purposes and as reminding system. Mind mapping is considered in more detail in Chapter 22.

There is also a wide range of software specifically for study skills and memory training. Two such programs developed by Jane Mitchell include 'Mastering Memory' and 'Time 2 Revise'/'Timely Reminders'. 'Mastering Memory' helps to improve short-term memory, enhances the learner's capacity to transfer new information to other areas of learning and enhances long-term retention (www.calsc.co.uk). 'Time 2 Revise'/'Timely

Reminders' are packages that can help to structure the revision process using mind maps, index cards, and revision notes. The emphasis is on encouraging the student to use the facts rather than rote-learning them. This active learning has been shown to be significantly more successful than passive learning in retention and recall, as well as in enhancing understanding. 'Lumosity' provides daily workouts that draw from more than 25 brain games to challenge five core cognitive abilities.

Provide external memory aids

Reminders can be provided for students in class, and it is important that if this is done, the memory aids are specifically task-related (not just wall posters that tend to blend into the background after a week or two). These could include:

- vocabulary lists
- spelling rules
- number lines
- manipulatives (hands-on materials)

Chapter 22: Active information processing

Pupils should be encouraged to practise actively organising information for retrieval – for instance, by using mind maps, bullet points and so on. These strategies should be explicitly taught. For many pupils, they do not come automatically but they certainly can be learned and are often very much appreciated because they can reduce stress and anxiety in students who are struggling to keep up as their volume of work increases. In this chapter we will look at four active processing techniques that can be used to improve recall:

- Repetition and overlearning
- Prioritising
- Organising information
- Mind mapping

Repetition and overlearning

Provide opportunities to reinforce the key points and also overlearning (reviewing materials already covered) to ensure that these points are consolidated and can later be recalled with ease. This can be achieved in a variety of ways and preferably not through conventional, and often tedious, rote-learning. In order to maximise the effect of repetition of learning, it is important that a multisensory mode of learning is utilised. Some learners may not remember information first time around, and rote repetition is not always effective. So, information should be repeated in a range of different ways. Memory cards, visuals, headings, summaries, notes and discussion are all helpful for overlearning. All these can be repeating the same information, but using various means to do it. This is how information is consolidated and mastered.

Prioritising

Prioritising involves deciding what to do first, and what is more (or less) important. Students often seem to have too much to learn, or so they might think! But feeling overburdened is common for students, particularly as the curriculum appears to be becoming more and more crammed and often students (even young students) have much more to learn than they have time for. Often, they have to be selective and make choices. We are surrounded by choices and decisions every day, and in everyday life it is necessary to prioritise. It is no different for students when they are studying, and they need to gain practice in doing this.

When students have a list of things to achieve, it can be difficult for them to decide what to do first and what is less important. This can apply to daily tasks as well as to specific areas of study. It is important that students are presented with dilemmas that require decisions to be made and obtain practice at prioritising the different tasks that have to be carried out. Prioritising actions can help to clear the mind of competing tasks to be carried out, and this will allow the student to focus exclusively on the task in hand and not worry about the other things that have to be done. Making a priority list is a good idea. This can help to reduce the burden of trying to read too much information for a piece of work, and also reduce the potential to become 'stressed out' by the quantity of material to be learned.

Organising information

This is important for memory. Many students concentrate on getting the information down on paper through note-taking and then at some later point they start to re-arrange it. This can be effective as the student is personalising the information to make it more meaningful to him- or herself. But it can be more effective if students can organise the information at the time of learning. That is, as they are making the notes, they should be arranging the information into some sort of meaningful manner. Not only is this a more efficient way to study, but it can also enhance comprehension. Using headings and sub-headings can help to organise the information, but also it can help to put it into some kind of meaningful context. The key to organising information is to re-arrange it in such a way that it can be more easily understood and retained.

How to help – organising information

☞ **Use headings and sub-headings** – these help to organise information. It should be possible for the student to go through pages of notes just looking at the headings and sub-headings and be able to understand the whole piece, and this is crucial for retention and recall. It is important to practice using heading and sub-headings.

☞ **Use visuals** – this helps to personalise the information, which is crucial for retention and recall.

☞ **Create mind maps** – this is a good way to use visuals. Mind maps can highlight the relationship between different facts and concepts. This technique can therefore help to give a deeper understanding of the subject and the connections between different aspects. These are discussed more fully below.

☞ **Chunking** – this is also an excellent strategy for organising information and can also help with retention. For example, if you are studying the geography of a country, make a 'chunk' of all the facts relating to climate. You should be able to chunk at least four items together, so find at least four items that have a strong connection.

☞ **Visualise** – it is more effective to use all your senses when learning. This means using the visual modality, and for some learners this is particularly important. Even if the learner is not naturally a visual person, a graphic or a symbol can still help to strengthen the memory trace.

☞ **Imagine** – one of the important aspects about memory is that it is very personal. Memory is individual, and the more individual it is, the more effective retention can be. That is why imagination can be useful. The use of imaginative images or connections can stamp a personal identity on the information to be remembered.

☞ **Active learning** – this can help the learner to retain and understand the new information to be learned. The more active the learner is, the more likely it is that the information will be understood and retained. This activity could be in the form of discussion, but it could also be in drama form and as a first-person speech. This can be done more easily in some subjects, such as History, where speeches and drama can be used to re-enact historical events.

> ☞ **Discussion** – for many learners, discussion is the most effective means of retaining and understanding information. Discussion can make the information meaningful and can help learners to experiment with ideas and views. It is this experimentation that helps learners extend their thinking and learning. For some, discussion can be like 'thinking aloud'.
>
> ☞ **Mnemonics** – these can be auditory or visual, or both auditory and visual. Auditory mnemonics may take the form of rhyming or alliteration, whereas visual mnemonics can be used by relating the material to be remembered to a familiar scene, such as the classroom.

Mind-mapping

Mind-mapping was developed by Tony Buzan (1993) to help children and adults to develop their learning skills, and utilise as much of their abilities as possible.[41] According to Buzan, a mind map is an expression of 'radiant thinking' and is therefore a natural function of the human mind. That is, he believes that our knowledge of a topic will naturally have a central theme, and other sub-themes will radiate (like beams of light from the sun) from it. It is a powerful graphic technique which provides a universal key to unlocking the potential of the brain.

Expert View

"Memory and creativity are essential to education, but if you teach memory incorrectly, it is a total waste of time, and it will inhibit learning."

Tony Buzan

Mind maps "help you to make a distinction between your mental storage capacity, which your mind map will help you demonstrate, and your mental storage efficiency, which your mind map will help you achieve". What Buzan is suggesting here is that that mind maps enable the learner to make the best use of the brain's capacity to hold and retrieve information – it's like giving learners the key to their library! The procedure is now widely used to extend memory capacity and develop lateral thinking.

Mind-mapping can be a simple or a sophisticated strategy, depending on how it is developed and used by the individual. It is used to help the learner to remember a considerable amount of information, and it encourages students to think of and develop the main ideas of a

---

41   Buzan T (1993) *The Mind Map Book*. London: BBC Books.

passage or material to be learned. It adopts in many ways some of the principles discussed earlier in this book in relation to schema theory (see Chapter 17). Essentially, mind maps are individual learning tools, and someone else's mind map may not be meaningful to another person. It is important, therefore, that children should create their own in order to help both understanding of key concepts and the retention and recall of associated facts.

Mind-mapping can help students to remember and organise information, and this exercise in itself can aid understanding. Elaborate versions of mind maps can be constructed using pictorial images, symbols and different colours. The following video link shows how mind-mapping is done: http://www.youtube.com/watch?v=MlabrWv25qQ.

How to help – creating a mind map

To **create a mind map**, it is best to start with a topic that is familiar to the student – such as a sport or hobby, or what they did at the weekend. The following procedure could be used:

- list everything you did at the weekend
- place the items into categories - family, friends, school, recreation, etc.
- make a central image in the middle of the page. This could be a picture of you, or a drawing representing the phrase 'my weekend'
- place all the categories around the image
- list all the people you saw at the weekend
- extend each of the categories into sub-categories – for example, for friends you might have sub-categories such as activities with friends, where they took place, conversations, etc.
- try to divide these groups further, e.g. 'activities with friends' could be divided into 'sport', 'cinema', etc, and for 'cinema', the specific film could be under another sub-heading
- once all the information has been put down into a mind map, additional images can be made to represent key words. These need not be works of art, but they should be made, or compiled, by you, and they should make sense to you.

Mind maps can be used to help the pupil engage with a topic, and later to remember content. The idea is that the mind map helps the student to remember the information and organise if for easier recall. It is also good practice in lateral thinking, because it helps the student to make connections and extend his or her thinking.

☞ **Other memory aids** that are useful and inexpensive are listed below. These can be valuable supporting resources for creating mind maps, but they also have broader potential to assist with revision in particular and learning in general.

- coloured writing and highlighting pens
- 'Post-it' notes in different shapes and colours
- paper in different colours
- a wall chart
- a cork board for checklists;
- 'Blu Tack' for attaching aides-memoire to objects
- index cards and a box for notes

Part 5: Essay-writing, exams and lifelong learning

Chapter 23: Planning and writing a good essay

As we have seen, effective learning requires a systematic approach, and this is equally important if the student is to be able to demonstrate that learning has been effective. Very often, this will be in the form of an essay, but the same principles will apply for things like project work. The student has to take steps to:

> **Key Point**
>
> *Effective learning requires a systematic approach, and this is equally important if the student is to be able to demonstrate that learning has been effective.*

- **understand** the task or information being presented
- **recognise** what the task involves, or the information is indicating
- **identify** the key points in the task or information
- **implement** the task, using the information provided
- **become 'autonomous'** in accessing the information and carrying out the task
- **be able to transfer** the new learning to other learning tasks

In an essay, the first four points above can be addressed by paying careful attention to the question or title. This will require a detailed and accurate form of reading. The learner will need to be aware of the type of questions that can be asked, and must be able to ask him- or herself questions about the question! The last two points are a reminder that, although the student might initially need support, he or she should be aiming to work independently using these techniques, so that they can be drawn upon in other settings (and, very importantly, in exams; exams are discussed more fully in Chapters 25-26).

It is important that students are able to express themselves when writing essays. Essay writing often involves adopting a more formal tone than is typically used when speaking, so students will need to be able to draw on more complex words and a wider vocabulary in order to achieve this. More descriptive words can also be a good way to draw the reader in and involve them in a piece of writing.

> ## How to help – extending vocabulary

> ☞ The following method can be used to increase students' vocabulary, in order to enable better expression in essays:
>
> As a template, take a colour shade card where, for example, all the yellow shades are shown. Now, ask pupils to write different 'shades' of the same word. So, for example, take the word 'make' and think of all the other words that have a similar meaning:
>
> - make...
> - create...
> - establish...
> - generate...
> - develop
>
> ☞ Another method for extending vocabulary might be to select some words, and ask the student to write different meanings for that word sound. For example:
>
> - sent = to deliver
> - cent = money
> - scent = smell
>
> This extends vocabulary, and can also help with spelling and word discrimination.

The essay writing process

Study the question

Teachers should encourage the student to think about the implications of the question/instructions, and to consider the information gleaned in different ways. Learners will need to take the time to consider:

- Where in the course does this topic come?
- What are the issues?
- What is actually being said/asked?
- What is required of me, and how will I know if I am right?

By doing this, it should become apparent to the student if the question has initially been misread or misunderstood.

Questioning also involves understanding the processing words usually used or implied in essay questions – for example, 'describe', 'contrast' 'evaluate', 'discuss', 'analyse'. Careful thought needs to be given to the terms that are used. More information on terms used in questions can be found in Chapters 25-26 on exams.

How to help – understanding essay questions

- An essay that asks a student to **'describe'** is looking for basic, surface knowledge – so he or she should provide a description of the topic. This might form the first part of a more complex piece of work.
- **'Contrast'** suggests that the student should be able to draw out characteristics of the items to be contrasted, and discuss where the key points of similarity or difference are.
- The word **'evaluate'** indicates that the student should be able to form a judgement about the topic – and, importantly, to defend that judgement by drawing on evidence, and not just the student's personal opinion.
- An invitation to **'discuss'** also implies some level of evaluation of the different characteristics or features of the topic that are of interest – again, providing evidence as to why they are of interest.
- If the essay title asks the student to **'analyse'** a topic, then he or she will be expected to be analytic – taking an in-depth, critical approach. Being critical does not mean criticising – it means not taking facts for granted, but always questioning them and again evidence is needed to support any argument.

Plan

Produce a skeleton outline of how to tackle the question. We can't stress enough how important this is. Often, we find that students will launch into a question, and then find themselves lost in a maze of points they would like to make, or at a dead end because their argument leads nowhere.

It's useful here to ask students to really think about the reader, and how he or she is going to be able to navigate their essay. The reader will need structure, and this includes a clear introduction, signposts and links between points, and a clear conclusion. The structure should orient to the question that was set – for example, if the student is asked to 'compare and contrast', the comparisons and contrasts must be clear to the reader.

The plan can be done using a mind map, or bulletpoints. Visual images can be used to help younger pupils. The learner can start with a small and personal topic that does not require additional reading – such as 'my weekend' – and develop some key headings with images. This can be developed into a mind map (a way of organising information that is more visual than simple text).

It's important to leave spaces to add information because often as the student is writing, he or she will remember additional points that should be made. When this happens – it's very important to go back to the plan, make a quick note of the point, then get back to the essay. This means that the student will be able to keep to the clear structure that was planned. The structure can of course be amended if, in the course of writing, it becomes clear that it doesn't match the arguments the student wants to make.

Collect information

In order to find the materials required, a number of processing skills have to be used – for example, sequencing, reading, summarising, critical note-taking and selection of sources. Much of this can be challenging, and information-gathering is discussed in more detail in Chapter 15. As much time as possible should be allowed for this stage. Being pressurised by time only makes the task more difficult. It is important to keep asking questions about the procedure – for example:

- "What exactly am I looking for?"
- "How much information do I need?"
- "Is this the most up-to-date account?"
- "Do I have evidence from both sides of the argument?"

Write the essay

This will be a lot easier to do when time has been spent on planning. It can also be helpful to use a checklist or template to check that all of the elements have been addressed, and we have provided one below.

Proof-reading and editing

Time needs to be allocated for this. It is preferable to leave a time gap between writing and proof-reading, because when we first read over our work, we often don't spot mistakes. We read what we thought we wrote. If time is limited, it can be helpful to read text aloud, or use text-reading software, because then the student might hear a mistake that he or she has not seen. Sometimes it can take several readings to proof-read effectively – but it is a good skill to have and practise at. This can pay real dividends, and it is worth stressing to students that many authors will draft and redraft several times as part of their writing process.

How to help – essay writing checklist

☞ When writing an essay, it is important to ensure that all necessary elements have been covered and addressed. Some suggested questions for inclusion in an essay-writing checklist are:

- Have I kept to the essay question?
- Does the introduction signal what I have done in the essay?
- Have I demonstrated that I have read and understood the texts/sources?
- Have I been analytical, critical and questioning?
- Does the essay flow logically?
- Have I linked the paragraphs?
- Does the conclusion show how I have developed the points?
- Have I included a reference section and bibliography?

Chapter 24: Effective revision

Approaching revision

The object of revision is not to memorise a complete course but rather to enhance understanding of the issues, and to be able to develop important points in written work. The key to success is organisation. This is important for many reasons. First, it will give the student a sense of control over the process.

> **Key Point**
>
> There is more to revising effectively for a test or exam than churning through past papers.

Second, it breaks the revision tasks down into manageable chunks, and this is more likely to lead to feelings of progress and eventual success. And third, it encourages an active approach that is more engaging and interesting, and therefore more likely to result in improved understanding and recall.

There is more to revising effectively for a test or exam than churning through past papers. This helps, of course, but there is very likely not enough coaching on how to undertake the test, and the type of techniques and strategies that can be helpful for the student. It is important to get the learning right and not to focus solely on the exam. Exam preparation is therefore best viewed from a perspective of learning strategies and learning skills. It is also essential that students take care of themselves during revision and over exam periods, in order to maximise the return on time spent studying.

Rest is best

Ellenbogen, Payne and Stickgold (2006) have researched the role of sleep in learning.[42] Their research suggests that sleep plays an important role in memory, both before and after learning a new task. They found that a sleep-deprived person cannot optimally focus attention, and therefore cannot learn efficiently, and that sleep itself has a role in the consolidation of memory. This is essential for learning new information, but it is also important for preparation and readiness for exams. They maintain that when we are sleep-deprived, our focus, attention, and vigilance drift, making it more difficult to receive information. Without

---

42 Ellenbogen M, Payne JD & Stickgold R (2006) The role of sleep in declarative memory consolidation: passive, permissive, active or none? *Curr Opin Neurobiol* 16(6): 716-22.

adequate sleep and rest, overworked neurons can no longer function to coordinate information properly, and we lose our ability to access previously learned information.

While there is little doubt that sleeping well during revision and exam periods benefits learning, it is not always easy to achieve. However, students should be mindful that getting adequate sleep on the nights leading up to an exam is far more important than last-minute bashing over notes. More information concerning sleep and its role in memory consolidation and the learning process can be found here: http://healthysleep.med.harvard.edu/healthy/matters/benefits-of-sleep/learning-memory.

Memory and understanding

On the subject of memory, it is important to note that memory should not be seen in isolation. Exams should not test memory. Rather, memory needs to be integrated into a study skills programme so that memory is taken in context to a problem or topic. The key point is that understanding aids memory. Without understanding, the memory trace will soon fade. Most of us, regardless of age, will benefit from a structure to help with memory, and we have already stressed the importance of students developing their own specific memory strategies. These strategies should include comprehension – it is crucial for the student to understand the material and develop concepts, for example by 'thinking around' the topic to appreciate its key points, how they relate to each other, and the relevance of the topic for the broader area of study.

Study management

The exam is the end product, but all the real work comes before then! Study management, in association with stress management, is the key to this. Some general recommendations for students are shown below:

- Make a short term and long-term study plan – and you need to start this quite a number of weeks before the exams. All exams need to be considered in the study plan, not only those that are imminent. So, as well as the urgent ones, you have to plan time to study topics for the more distant exams in the current exam schedule.
- Set times for each subject and topic – try not to leave a subject or topic too long. It is a good idea to study a little of each subject most days so, for example, in a three-day period all subjects will have been touched on in some way. Even if it is just a passing reference – the seed has

been planted, and your brain may well be working on this without you realising it!

- Find your space – this can help you feel comfortable when you are studying. Know what you are looking for in a study place. Do you prefer complete quiet, ambient background noise or music? Does the location have comfortable seats, or libraries with the reference books you need access to? Everyone has their own idea of what is best for them, but it is important that students think about this and make a deliberate choice if they have the opportunity.

- Check your stationery needs – consider the types of notebooks and study planners available. Some students may simply need sticky notes, whereas others may prefer a more sophisticated study planner. Coloured pens and highlighters can help to make information more visually memorable.

- Try to build some slack into your schedule – there is a great danger of students filling their schedule to the brim, and as a result it becomes unmanageable. Leave time for friends and your favourite TV programme. Don't put your personal life on hold 100% of the time; strike a sensible balance.

- During study, give yourself 'brain breaks' – if you feel you are re-reading a text and not fully taking it in, then stop and go for a walk. Brain breaks are important – some students may be able to work for a morning without a break, while others may need a break every thirty minutes or so. There is nothing wrong with that – put it down to individual differences. Students should acknowledge and respect their own study patterns.

- Your health is important – eat well during the run up to exams. Good nourishment gives you sustained energy and makes you feel better. Eat a good balance of foods – not all snack foods, which can be tempting, but a variety of different foods. Preparing a meal can also be a brain break.

How to help – 'The Five Rs' of effective revision

☞ Students often remember the revision process better if they have an acronym, such as the one below (adapted from Reid & Green, 2009):[43]

- **Recognise** – identify your own preferred way of learning.
- **Revise** the information that is to be learned. The important point is that this revision can take a number of different forms, but will work more effectively if there is a revision plan and timetable.
- **Review** – this is important as it is the reviewing that consolidates memory and ensures understanding and retention in long-term memory. This will make it easier to remember.
- **Recall** – this also needs to be practised; simply, the more you use a skill or piece of information, the more easily it will be memorised and recalled in future use.
- **Reflect** – this this can be done through the use of reflective questions such as 'Why?' and 'How?', but also through thinking and even thinking aloud. Reflection is important for effective learning, and to help learners become more efficient, so that they can use an effective strategy the next time they are learning something similar.

Planning revision

A revision plan should be made in detail. For each topic, a programme of multisensory study should be undertaken. Revision has to be an active process, and not a passive one of just reading and re-reading text. It is possible to identify a number of helpful steps to get started:

- **Step 1** – collect and compile notes for the topic. Check that class notes are complete. Check that all of the recommended reading has been done, and notes are taken. Check comprehension – never try to memorise information that is not understood. It can help if the student breaks down complex ideas and puts them into his or her own words.
- **Step 2** – dictate the key points and issues using a digital recorder, phone or computer.

---

43 Reid G & Green S (2009) *Effective Learning*. London: Continuum International Publishing Group.

- **Step 3** – listen to information gathered on the recording.
- **Step 4** – listen a second time, but on this occasion, enter the information on a prepared mind map or diagram.
- **Step 5** – write linear notes from the diagram.
- **Step 6** – put key words and facts for each section on index cards.
- **Step 7** – put topic titles and three or four headings on an index card.

How to help – creating a revision plan

☞ It is worthwhile taking a bit of time to reflect on how to plan the revision plan! By this, we mean that the pupil should think about what has helped him or her in the past, and what his or her individual learning preferences are. The following table could be used:

Activity	Things that help	Things to avoid
Reading		
Spelling		
Creative writing		
Answering test questions		
Remembering information		
Thinking		
Organisation		
Using spare time		
Solving difficult problems e.g. Maths		

☞ It is a good idea for the student to develop a study plan in the two weeks prior to the exams. It should be a simple one, such as the example below:

Topic	Part of topic	Questions on topic

☞ They can also make up an at-a-glance exam planner that they can refer to daily:

My Exam Planner		
Topics/subject to study	Part of the topic	Study plan
Environmental Studies	Climate change – arctic region	1. locate a good map
		2. note key areas
		3. obtain some facts on the area
		4. potential effect of climate change on area

My 'to-do' list

Make a list of possible questions on topic

Write opening paragraphs on topic

Note key people and events in each topic

Watch YouTube video on topic

Consider management of climate change at local level and national and international levels

Self-quizzing

As we have seen in previous chapters, self-questioning is a good strategy for developing effective and independent learning. Simply by making up questions, students are thinking about the type of questions they may be asked in assessments, so it is very good early preparation for exams. It can be helpful to write questions on a card, with answers on the back. The student goes through the questions, and the ones he or she gets wrong go to the top. This way, priority is given to the material that needs more attention.

There are various types of software that can be used to help in this process. For example, 'Quislet' is a customisable study tool available in both online and as an app. Users create customisable 'sets' using terms and definitions relating to virtually any subject. It provides a number of teaching tools to transform these sets into flashcards, quizzes and tests, or mini-games designed to familiarise users with their study terms (https://quislet.com/en-gb).

Discussion

For many learners, discussion is the best way to retain and understand information. Discussion can make the information meaningful, and it can help the learner to experiment with ideas and views. It is this experimentation that helps the learner extend his or her thinking and learning. For some learners, discussion can be like thinking aloud.

It is important that there are opportunities for discussion – it may be useful to actually timetable discussion time and split the class into smaller groups. It can be useful to work with a 'learning buddy', especially if the learner has difficulty in asking the right questions of him- or herself. Sharing information and questions with a learning buddy can be a way round this. Usually, each of the students will have something to contribute, and both will learn something from this type of exchange. The idea is that one of the students has a list of topics, and the other asks questions about that topic. They then take turns at asking the questions. For example, if the topic was 'Evolution', the other person could ask:

- What is meant by evolution?
- Can you explain how evolution works?
- Where do we get our evidence from?
- What is meant by divergent, convergent, and parallel evolution?
- Why is evolution important?

When the person answers these questions, it is important for the other person to question his or her response. This will ensure that both are thinking critically about the topic.

Chapter 25: Exam preparation

The challenge of exams

Examinations can cause considerable anxiety for many students. Putwain (2008a) maintains that there has been a significant increase in interest in exam stress and test anxiety in the UK.[44] He argues that this is due partly to the policy of using students' performance in high-stakes tests, such as Year 6 SATs (Standard Attainment Tests) and GCSEs (General Certificate of Secondary Education exams) as measures of school and teacher accountability. This, he believes, has resulted in an 'audit culture' in schools. That is, schools might focus on their need to provide evidence for school inspectors, and this can restrict teachers' autonomy in deciding how best to teach their pupils, mark their work and record their learning. Putwain also argues that the UK Government agenda for England, Wales and Northern Ireland, 'Every Child Matters' (since renamed 'Help Children Achieve More'), positions schools as being responsible for the mental wellbeing of their students. Therefore, the issue of stress and anxiety in relation to examinations is being taken more seriously now than before.

Expert View

"Given the current climate of increasing the amount of high stakes testing in children, debates around the issue of test anxiety and examination stress are unlikely to go away."

Dave Putwain

A study skills programme aimed at exam revision techniques can help students to revise effectively, and to use their available time efficiently. Many students spend a considerable length of time revising, and have a good grasp of the subject, but still fall down when it comes to the day of the exam. If the efforts made by these students are to be rewarded, guidance and support in study techniques will be just as crucial as knowledge and understanding of the subject itself. In fact, Putwain shows that many highly test-anxious students make more effort than those with low test anxiety, as a compensatory mechanism.[44] He discusses the value of using more assessed course work as a means of tackling exam anxiety, on the basis that students would find coursework less stressful than exams.[45] However, he argues that this fails to take into account the fact

---

44   Putwain DW (2008a) Examination stress and test anxiety. *Psychologist* 21(12): 1,026–29.
45   Putwain DW (2008b) Supporting assessment stress in key stage 4 students. *Educ Studies* 34(2): 83–95.

that coursework has its own forms of stress that might cause just as much anxiety to some students as examinations. These include:

- The diverse skills involved in managing projects, such as data collection, literature reviewing and group work, perhaps without any real prior experience
- Having to stay up late to meet deadlines, and managing workload
- Having to work on several coursework projects simultaneously while doing other schoolwork and preparing for exams

Another possible alternative to exams is to use more teacher-based judgements that are based on factors other than test results. This approach has come to prominence out of necessity during the COVID-19 pandemic. But, as Putwain argues, this can raise questions about consistency, and it will be difficult to ensure reliability and comparability of the measures used.[45] So, the issue raised in the very first chapter of this book remains – does the focus on testing encourage shallow learning and performance goals, at the expense of deep learning and mastery goals?

Managing exam stress

Anxiety and stress concerning tests and exams is unfortunately a reality for many students, and there is no doubt that it can have a detrimental effect on performance and results. Zeidner (1998) outlines three components of test anxiety.[46] These are:

- **Behavioural** – for example, poor study skills, avoidance of work and procrastination, and being stuck in a 'learned helplessness' cycle. This describes the situation where the learner has come to believe that whatever he or she does will have no effective or useful outcome, so the logical thing to do is to stop trying.
- **Cognitive** – that is, negative thoughts can occur in relation to exams (e.g. *"If I fail this exam, my whole life is a failure"*) and the 'performance-inhibiting' difficulties that may arise from anxiety (e.g. problems in recalling facts and difficulty in reading and understanding questions).
- **Emotional/affective** – this relates to the person's self-appraisal of his or her physiological state, and could include tension, stomach upset and exam fright.

---

46 Zeidner M (1998) *Test Anxiety: The State Of The Art*. New York: Plenum.

There is no simple panacea for exam stress; however, there are a number of positive strategies that can serve to prevent anxiety from becoming too severe and help learners to achieve full recognition for their efforts. The first step is to identify those students who are anxious or at risk of becoming anxious, and this is important because anxiety can often be covered up.

Putwain (2008a) suggests that early identification of highly test-anxious students is very difficult, but teachers can look out for warning signs, such as procrastination and a surprising loss of interest in academic work.[44] He also argues that we can change the test conditions by making exams less stressful. For example, more breaks and a smaller venue may be useful and less intimidating. It might be more effective if reducing anxiety becomes the main target, along with developing academic self-esteem. At the same time, there is still an important role for programmes and strategies that can improve study and test-taking skills.

There is a view that exam anxiety may be highly correlated to other factors, such as achievement goals and academic self-concept. This means that exam stress should perhaps be dealt with from a more holistic and not purely situational perspective. Working with the student to develop a more positive academic self-concept may pay off when it comes to exam time. This type of intervention should start well before the exam, and preferably as early as possible in the student's schooling. In support of this view, Putwain did find that both academic self-concept and perceived test competence are negatively related to test anxiety. That is, the better the student's self-concept and belief that he or she can manage well in tests, the less anxiety there will be (and vice-versa).[44]

Key Point

Working with the student to develop a more positive academic self-concept may pay off when it comes to exam time.

How to help – exam stress management

Many of the points that we have already discussed in this book – such as good diet, brain breaks, social outlets and a study planner - can help to keep anxiety related to tests and examinations under control. Effective stress management is a blend of direct action (addressing the problem) and palliative activities (restorative relaxation), and both are important. There may be a tendency for some students to put too much weight on the direct action side, but it is also important that they achieve a balance and give themselves the opportunity for more relaxation-based activities.

☞ **Direct action for stress**

Direct action involves tangible activities that can certainly provide the impression that the student is dealing with the potential stressors, and this can have the desired effect of improving academic self-esteem. It could include a study skills programme and targeted study. That is, direct action means actively dealing with the perceived problem. This includes:

- techniques to help with reading exam questions and answering these questions.
- effective reading – asking the right questions while reading.
- developing note-taking skills.
- developing strategies for organisation and retention, such as mind mapping and spider diagrams.
- developing techniques for expressive writing, such as paragraph writing skills, writing opening paragraphs and planning the answer to exam questions, and writing frameworks prior to answering questions.

☞ **Palliative activities for stress**

Palliative activities are approaches that are synonymous with relaxation. The aim is to restore the body so that the person is more resilient, and more able to cope with stressors! Although it may be difficult for some, time has to be allocated for a form of relaxation. It is important to note that there is no hierarchy of palliative approaches – it in entirely up to the individual, as it really comes down to personal preference. Some of the more popular palliative approaches are:

- **Simple, deep breathing exercises** – the recommended method is breathing in through your nose and out through your mouth. You should try to inhale enough so that your lower abdomen rises and falls, and count slowly as you exhale.
- **Progressive muscle relaxation** – this involves systematically tensing and relaxing different muscle groups in the body. It is a good idea to do this to relaxing background music.
- **Mindfulness meditation** – this is a popular method, and involves switching off from the past and the future, and focusing on the here and now. In order to do this effectively, you need to have a focus – either internal (such as your breathing rhythm) or external (such as a candle or an object in the room).
- **Yoga** – this is also very popular and very effective. It is a gentle way of reducing stress, and can be suitable for everyone irrespective of fitness level or age. Tai Chi is an alternative, and this is also very effective. It involves similar movements to yoga with an emphasis on control of body and mind.
- **Massage** – this can be very relaxing. It can rid the body of tensions and create a good feeling of wellbeing.

Anxiety – good or bad?

It is generally accepted that anxiety can be disadvantageous and result in lower levels of performance. While this can be true, it is also known that a certain level of anxiety can be motivating and stimulating. This is because our body speeds up into a state of readiness. For example, for professional football players before a game a certain level of anxiety can give them the edge and prepare them to perform at their best, but there does come a tipping point where too much anxiety can be counterproductive. The danger point is when anxiety persists after the challenge has passed. As Reilly (2015) points out, this can result in physical and cognitive reactions such as:[47]

- fast heart rate
- excessive sweating
- disturbed sleep
- concentration difficulties

---

47 Reilly N (2015) *Anxiety And Depression In The Classroom: A Teacher's Guide to Fostering Self-Regulation in Young Students*. London: WW Norton Publishers.

- catastrophic thinking and irrational thinking
- mood swings
- high level of nervousness and a tendency to avoid new challenges

It is therefore good practice to look out for those danger signs, and to ensure that any anxiety levels are kept under control and remain manageable.

How to help – anxiety prevention checklist

☞ Identifying risks of anxiety among learners is essential if stress levels are to be kept in check and any anxiety is to be a positive rather than a negative force. Below are some suggestions:

- Is the learner fully aware of the requirements of the task?
- Is the vocabulary at the appropriate level for the learner?
- Does the learner feel comfortable in the learning environment?
- If working in a group, are the group dynamics okay?
- Is the task multisensory – with visual and kinaesthetic activities, as well as written ones? Does the task build on the learner's successes?
- Has the learner's previous knowledge of the task been taken into account?
- Will immediate positive feedback to the learner be possible?
- Does the learner appear anxious about the task? (consider facial expression, body language)
- Is the task structured for the learner?

Chapter 26: Sitting the exam

Preparation

Most wise people will readily suggest that the student should relax the day before an exam. For some, this may be good advice, but many find it difficult to switch off from thinking about the next day's challenges. In this case, some light revision can be undertaken. It is important that this should not be new information, but gently going over what the student already knows, perhaps in a different context – for example, sitting in the park or walking and mentally answering some questions (the student might find it helpful to talk to him- or herself about how he or she could respond to a question; this provides a good auditory memory). It is a good idea to have a list of possible questions to refer to if walking or just sitting in pleasant surroundings.

> **Key Point**
>
> It is advantageous to feel good before you arrive at the exam room – feel good, do good!

It is also important to keep your energies at an optimum level during the exam period. Morris (2020) suggests that staying hydrated when studying and throughout an exam period is fundamental.[48] A dehydration level of as little as one to two per cent will bring about unhelpful side-effects for performance (loss of concentration, moodiness and headaches). If the student can manage his or her hydration, nutrition, rest and recovery throughout the exam period then then this will help to reduce stress levels and maximise performance.

Morning routine

If one asks professional sportsmen about their morning routine prior to a major event – or even non-professionals doing a local run or bike event – one will often find that they have a routine. It may be a well-practised one, and it will be one they have thought about and are able to stick to. There are many variations of this, but one general point is: no rushing, and no flustering! Spend a moment relaxing or sitting quietly, with no interruption – some may prefer to listen to soothing or inspiring music. It is important that students leave themselves plenty of time to do the things they need to do in the morning. It is advantageous to feel good before you arrive at the exam room – feel good, do good!

---

48 Morris A (2020) *How Can Students Manage Their Energy Levels During An Exam Period?* London, UK: Believe Perform. Available at: https://believeperform.com/how-can-studentsmanage-their-energy-levels-during-exam-period/ [last accessed January 2021]

The exam room

Before the exam begins, it is important to listen carefully to the exam invigilator for instructions. Although these instructions are usually fairly standard, listening carefully can help the student focus, and that is a good start – like a warm-up. The student should have already considered how to use the time and worked out how much time to allocate for each question. It is important to plan this, and to stick to the plan.

Dealing with exam questions

In order to help you relax when faced with the exam script, a good tip is to immediately scan through the entire exam paper. Allow some time for this. The sequence is:

- Read through the exam paper
- Note the suggested time for each section and points value for each question.
- Determine if you have to complete the questions in a certain order.
- Tick all the questions in the paper you think you can attempt.
- Decide the order you are going to tackle the questions.
- Make a firm decision on the question you are tackling first.
- For essay questions, write a mini-outline of your answer – use bullet points, headings and sub-headings.
- Remember – do not overspend time on one question. Ensure you have decided how much time you can allocate to each question, and keep to that time. This is very important.
- Do not hesitate to complete a question quickly in order to keep to your time, even if this means you shorten your conclusion to a single sentence.
- When budgeting your time, try to allow time at the end to double check your answers. This may not always be possible, but you should try to do it.
- After the exam, you will be tired and relieved. But try to use a little time soon after the exam to reflect on your exam strategy, and perhaps what you might do differently next time.

Question keywords

Many students do not seem to spend sufficient time studying the question. This can account for unexpectedly low grades. It is crucial, therefore, that the student gives him- or herself sufficient time to read the question carefully and read it several times again while writing the response. It is important that key words are underlined, and the student should not hesitate to mark or underline those points on the exam paper. An example is shown below, with key words highlighted.

How to help – exam question keywords

☞ Question:
*How do you **explain** the **difference** in Lady Macbeth's **manner** towards Macbeth after **the Banquo ghost scene** (Act 3, Scene 4), as compared with her bearing after **the murder of Duncan** (Act 2, Scene 2)?*

- **explain** – the student should provide an explanation, not a narrative or an account but an explanation, so the examiner can say "Aah I see, okay."
- **difference** – this means that there should be some contrasting points, and the student needs to make these points clear in order to show that there was in fact a difference.
- **manner** – this word needs teasing out; what do we mean by manner?
- **two events** are mentioned – these need to be briefly described as a preamble to the contrast. It is important that the contrast (i.e. the difference) should be dominant throughout the answer.

Question selection

It is interesting that students may take a lengthy time to decide on which computer or tablet to buy to assist with their studies, but when it comes to exam questions they may respond in haste without sufficient thought. Yet this choice can have a significant impact on the overall grade achieved in the exam, and potentially on students' future education and careers. They obviously need to read through all the questions – assuming they have studied the full course – and do the following:

- Read over all the questions and note the general content area of each one
- Select at least two questions in the content you are most comfortable with
- Take one question at a time and mark down some rough notes, for example:
  - What is the question really asking?
  - What are the key points?
  - What areas have I studied that can be used?
  - Can I think now of how I might conclude this question?

The final point is very important because it will give the student direction and a focus for their whole answer. The student will be collecting evidence to steer him or her in the direction of the conclusion. This will help to avoid lengthy, page-filling narrative. It is likely the response to the question will be more direct. Once the student has made these rough notes for two questions, he or she should then decide which one to opt for. It is good to have a choice, but once the decision is made – that's it! It is crucially important that students do not change their mind once they have started a question. This wastes time and can cause confusion and panic. That is why it is important to carry out the pre-selection process quite thoroughly.

Timing and pacing

This is also very important – exams are not a race, but they are timed! The pacing of each of the questions can be worked out well in advance – the student will know the length of the exam and the number of questions, so that is the easy part. The more challenging aspect is the pacing involved in the answer. For that reason, it is crucial to produce a plan of the answer. In this plan, the student needs to note the key areas and the structure of the answer. They may note the following:

- Introduction – this should outline three or four points to be made in the body of the essay, and in this part the student should also allude to the conclusion
- Point 1
- Point 2
- Point 3
- Conclusion

It is important that each of these parts is considered equally. Often students spend too much time on one part and rush through the others. It is important that they divide their time equally. Some further discussion on answering questions is detailed below.

Answering the question

Questions do not deliberately seek to trick students, but some can be tricky! Again, it is important for the student to think hard about what the question is asking them to do, and to keep that in mind throughout the answer. Students need to be explicitly taught the language of assessment, because this can represent a barrier for many of them. Don't assume that all pupils will understand even the basic words. Some, for example, may have difficulty with specialist exam nouns like 'text', 'extract', 'source' or 'feature'. Students also need to understand all the command words (such as 'explain' and 'summarise'). Table 6 below (adapted from 'Closing the Word Gap', teachit.co.uk) shows terms that are commonly used in different exam boards in England. More information on terms used in questions can be found in Chapter 23 on essay writing.

Table 6: Terms used in exams

Common words used in exams	Exam Board		
	GCSE	AQA	Edexcel
Analyse	Yes		Yes
Comment	Yes		
Compare	Yes	Yes	Yes
Consider	Yes	Yes	Yes
Convey	Yes	Yes	
Describe	Yes	Yes	
Discuss	Yes		
Effect(s)	Yes	Yes	
Evaluate	Yes	Yes	Yes
Explain	Yes	Yes	Yes
Explore	Yes	Yes	Yes
Extract	Yes	Yes	Yes
Features	Yes	Yes	
Identify	Yes		Yes
Indicate	Yes		Yes
Insert	Yes	Yes	Yes
Methods	Yes	Yes	
Passage	Yes	Yes	
Persuade	Yes	Yes	

Present	Yes		
Refer	Yes	Yes	Yes
Reference	Yes	Yes	Yes
Respond	Yes	Yes	Yes
Section	Yes	Yes	
Similarities	Yes		Yes
Source	Yes	Yes	
Summary	Yes	Yes	
Support	Yes	Yes	Yes
Text	Yes	Yes	Yes

How to help – common types of exam question

☞ **Analyse** – this means that students should explore the main ideas of the subject or topic. They have to show why these ideas are important, but specifically how they are related to each other. Essentially, the student must dissect the topic. This can be tricky, and it is easy to go off on a tangent. It is therefore a good idea for the student to jot down the key points here to make sure that he or she stays on track.

☞ **Compare** – this means that the student should show the similarities and differences between different aspects of the topic. An important trap for students to be aware of is that they should not simply provide a narrative description of each of the areas. They must provide points of comparison, and it is important to keep this in mind at all times. They could try practising this with topics they are familiar with – e.g. compare soccer with rugby, or jazz with rap music. A structure for comparison questions is helpful – for soccer and rugby it might be rules, ball, scoring and team composition; for jazz and rap it might be instruments, styles, rhythms and song structures.

☞ **Discuss** – discussion means exactly that. In some ways, this is more challenging because students have to come up with their own points that they feel are important in the topic. They need to explore the topic by looking at the advantages and disadvantages, the arguments for and against, and attempt to come to some sort of opinion. Again, they will benefit from a structure for this.

> **Explain** – as indicated earlier, the answer should provide a clear response, and show why the key points are important. The response needs to make the topic accessible to the reader, and as far as possible by using clear examples.

> **Summarise** – this is a very important aspect in relation to answering exam questions and preparing for exams. Being able to summarise indicates that the student has understood the topic. A summary should provide a brief account of the main points and attempt to come to some conclusion, perhaps noting why the conclusion has been reached.

Issues around multiple-choice questions

Some exam questions can be very tricky, but multiple-choice questions can be deceptively tricky. First, there is usually quite a bit of reading to be done in this type of exam, and often it is a race against the clock to do it. This means that the student cannot spend too much time on any one response. There are some basic strategies that can help when tackling multiple-choice exams. These include:

- Read through all the possible responses quickly
- Note at least two you can discount quite quickly
- Read the remaining two (assuming there are four possibilities) in some detail
- Be positive, select one and note to yourself why you think that one is the correct answer.

Pacing in multiple-choice exams is vitally important. Keep monitoring your time – if you are allowing two minutes for each question, then it is important to stick to that. It is also important to get as much practice as possible in doing multiple-choice exams. They are quite different from other exams, and in many ways new exam skills have to be learned.

Reflecting and reviewing

It is important to get the importance of reflection across to every student. Many students feel that exams are for writing, and often comment on how much they wrote for an answer. Yet the quality of the response is often judged by the amount of reflection time the student puts in. The pace of the curriculum and often the exam schedule is such that we do not always actually encourage reflection, and the learners themselves can feel that time spent thinking is time wasted!

Reflection is an important aspect of learning, and it is crucial that learners are encouraged to do this. For many, it may not come easily, and the reflection will need to be structured for them. But it is an essential component of learning, and certainly of exams. The example below can be practised by learners of all ages, and will prepare them better for eventual exams.

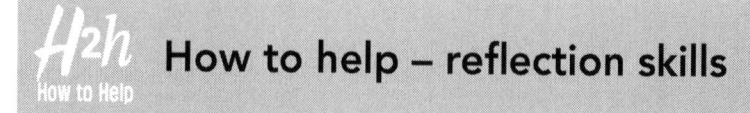

How to help – reflection skills

☞ Before the task, ask:
- What is my goal?
- What do I want to accomplish?
- What do I need?
- What is my deadline?

☞ During the task, ask:
- How am I doing?
- Do I need other resources?
- What else can I do?

☞ After task completion, ask:
- Did I accomplish my goal?
- Was I efficient?
- What worked?
- What didn't work?
- Why didn't it work?

The day after!

It is important to relax after an exam. No exam 'post-mortem' – forget about it if possible. That may be easier said than done, as people are likely to ask you how you got on. This is very well-meaning, but try to make your response quite general and polite, e.g. *"Well, it was tough, but I did my best"*; *"Some unexpected questions came up – but I still tackled them"*; *"I think I did okay, but I'd rather not think about it now."* It is important for the student to find a way to 'switch off' after the exam. This may not be too easy as students are likely to be really keyed up. They should give this some thought before the exam, as it can be a motivating factor if they know they will be able to do certain things afterwards that they cannot do as fully while preparing for the exam. They should make up a list of things they will do after the exam.

It is also important for students to celebrate after the exam – not when they get the results, but when they have completed the exam. That is the achievement! It is important for them to do something memorable such as attending a gig, going on holiday or just self-pampering – something they may not normally do.

How to help – top five after-exam activities

- Get lost! It is important to get re-absorbed in something different, such as a book or a television series – get a box set and re-absorb! This form of digression is excellent for moving on from an exam.
- Spend time with your friends and family, or take the opportunity to join a new group or club. This can also help you to shift your focus from the exam.
- Remember to 'clear the decks' – tidy your study area, place books and notes in neat files, and clear them off your shelves. This can be therapeutic in itself.
- Have some down time to yourself. This can be in the form of a special treat – doing something you'd like to do, going swimming or to the gym, or even just visiting a café and reading a book. Give your brain a break!
- Yoga and meditation – these are excellent for winding down and switching off.

Chapter 27: Lifelong learning

This chapter will focus on learning beyond school, and the skills required to cope with learning demands in Further Education (FE), Higher Education (HE) and the workplace. Many of the points made here have been discussed in earlier chapters – the same principles, skills and strategies are important throughout an individual's schooling, later education and the workplace.

> **Key Point**
>
> We always need to be aware that exam preparation does not prepare young people for life.

The key message of this chapter is that we always need to be aware that exam preparation does not prepare young people for life. It is therefore important that study skills incorporate problem-solving activities that can prepare them for learning beyond school. It is also important that young people are prepared to take advice at college and in the workplace, and to seek appropriate support where available.

Challenges in Further and Higher Education

Most colleges and universities are quite well-equipped to provide support to all students, including those who may have difficulties with the demands of the course. Each university will have its own specific guidelines and processes for students to follow. It is important, however, that these guidelines are well publicised, and that the student is left in no doubt about what type of action he or she needs to take. Some of the important stages can include a preliminary talk with the Course Tutor or Studies Advisor. This would help the student articulate his or her concerns, and the Course Tutor can advise on the most appropriate course of action. This would likely start with a preliminary meeting with the Student Advisory Service or equivalent. Each university will have a student support service, and they will be able to listen to the student's concerns and make some decisions on the best course of action.

Some of the challenges that students can experience in Higher Education relate to:

Reading accuracy and reading speed

In Higher Education there is often more reading than students are accustomed to, and this can result in a feeling of being overwhelmed. Some students can have difficulty in using their reading time effectively, and may not know how to scan a text to find out if it will be useful for them. Practice in scanning and skimming text and using the index and contents effectively is very useful for all students. These strategies are discussed more fully in Chapter 15. They will often need to re-read for full meaning, but some students can feel despondent when they do not grasp the meaning of a text first time. They may complain they have to re-read lots of times to get the meaning. However, this is not unusual, and students should expect to have to re-read and allow time for it.

Noting inferences in texts

Noting inferences in texts is important because it can give you insights into the key points in the passage or chapter. Some inferences can be detected quite easily – for example, *"When we arrived back home, we noticed that our dog had newsprint on his paws. We found the bedroom floor covered with tiny pieces of newspaper. We inferred that our dog had chewed the newspaper."* However, some words can infer a meaning that appears to conflict with what is expected. For example, the word 'smiling' can mean good or not so good, depending on the context. Predicting and inferring are different, and can be easily confused. Predicting is essentially asking what might happen next based on what we already know from the text. Inferring is looking at what the author really means and the hidden motive.

Understanding technical and/or subject-specific words

Technical words, or words that are specific to one subject area, can be challenging, particularly as many of them may look or sound similar, and they are not used in everyday language. Some examples of subject-specific vocabulary are shown below.

Table 7: Subject-specific terminology

History	Geography	Chemistry	Biology	Modern Languages
revolution	terrain	compound	stem	
epoch	climate	state	physiological	accent
dynasty	environment	experiment	cell	culture
			mutation	customs

English	Mathematics	Art	Music	P.E.
metaphor	calculate	textural	score	offside
literature	fraction	juxtaposed	orchestra	substitute
syntax	formulae	symbolise	cadence	marginal gain

Planning and organising written work

Many students just want to write, and often will put down almost everything they know about the topic, or the question. In order to ensure focus it is important that they pay some attention to, and spend some time on, planning. This is discussed elsewhere in this book.

How to help – writing frames

☞ A writing frame is a template that provides a scaffold for children's writing. Key words or phrases are included in a given order, allowing children to focus on what they want to say rather than spending time on the structure and form. An example is shown below.

Argument:

I think that _____ because _____.

The reasons for my thinking this are, first, _____.

Another reason is _____.

Moreover, _____ because _____.

These (facts/arguments/ideas) show that _____.

Some people think that _____, because

they argue that _____.

Discussion:

Another group who agree with this point of view are _____.

They say that _____.

On the other hand, _____.

They disagree with the idea that _____.

They claim that _____.

They also say _____.

My opinion is _____.

The reason for this is _____.

Memorising facts

It is important for students to appreciate that learning is not all memory. In fact, very little of it is! It is about understanding. They should refer to Bloom's Taxonomy. A good example of this can be seen in the following website: https://www.teachthought.com/learning/what-is-blooms-taxonomy-a-definition-for-teachers/.

Ideally, what students should be aiming for is the evaluation part of the taxonomy – that is, making and defending judgements that are based on the evidence. They can practise this with some common issues in today's society – for example, "Should cars be banned from city centres?" There are many topics they can practise with, irrespective of their background knowledge of the subject. They need practice in arguing their point on paper, rather than rephrasing what it might say in the book. Going further, they need to justify why the author might take a certain perspective, and probe more deeply to explore the authors viewpoints. Some general suggestions for memorising information are shown below:

- **Repetition** – opportunities for repetition are helpful and can relate to the need for over-learning.

- **Prioritising** – this involves deciding what to do first and what is less important. It can apply to daily tasks as well as to specific areas of study. This can help to reduce the burden of remembering a lot of information at the same time.

- **Organising information** – this is important for memory. The key to organising information is to re-arrange the information so it can be more easily understood and retained. Headings and sub-headings are helpful in organising information. Visuals can also re-enforce this. This helps to personalise the information, and personalising information is crucial for retention and recall.

- **Mind-mapping** – this can be useful because it is a good way to use visuals, and it also help with organisation. Mind maps can also show the relationships between different facts and concepts, and therefore can help to give a deeper understanding of the subject and the connections between different aspects.

- **Chunking** is also an excellent strategy for organising information. This involves grouping similar items or topics together, and this helps the student to understand and remember information.

- **Note-taking** – this can be a time-consuming exercise for students, and it may also turn out to be quite wasteful in terms of time. Students will need to practise and perhaps receive some guidance in note-taking. It will be helpful if they receive a handout of the lecture (preferably in advance of the lecture), but they will need practice in note-taking from books. An example is shown below.

How to help – taking notes from books

☞ The **Dysguise Structured Sequential System (DSSS)** is a method for maximising efficiency and effectiveness when students are taking notes from books. These are the steps:

- Read the contents, and the author biography. This can give you a schema.
- From the contents, decide which chapters you think will be useful.
- Consider the questions you want answered, and which chapters will answer those questions.
- Make a list of the possible questions – these should be in your mind when you are reading the chapter.
- Have a quick first read through the chapter, to get the general idea of the chapter.
- Marker pen or notepad at the ready – mark or note, in not more than four words at a time, some key points from the chapter.
- List those key points in your notepad – you can add to this by drawing a symbol, or using symbols or single words as a memory aid.
- Now read the chapter again – this time your aim is to embellish your key points. Look for some specific evidence to indicate why the points you have noted are indeed key points.
- Now, add evidence to your list of key points – go through your questions, and try to be as specific as possible, using the list you wrote earlier. Underline the important points from the evidence and answers to your questions.
- Finally, summarise the chapter using your notes and then file what you have created carefully – it is important to keep clearly labelled notes.

Empowerment

It is important that individuals of any age are able to stand up for themselves and ask the right type of questions to ensure that their needs – whatever these might be – are met. Empowerment is therefore very important, and it can be developed from the following:

- **Self-understanding** – students need to have an understanding of their strengths and difficulties, how they affects them and their performance, and what they need to do about to improve.
- **Understanding of others**, particularly tutors and employers – encouragement is needed to develop self-advocacy, and this can from friends, family or employers. There needs to be an awareness that training is important for any task, that all learners will need training, and that some may take longer to achieve the desired level of competence.
- **Support and a supportive environment** – at College in particular, this can involve support with the following:
  - **Organisation** of work area and of workload
  - **Reading strategies** – and particularly reading speed and strategies for skimming and scanning
  - **Note-taking and filing** – and being able to organise and make sense of notes and be able to access these later
  - **Listening to instructions** – and not to feel embarrassed to ask them to be repeated, or to write them down
  - **Making presentations** – this can be an ordeal for many students, regardless of their abilities. Being able to identify the key points is a good starter for this – even if the student just reviewed the key points, this could turn into a competent presentation.

Careers advice

Careers guidance/counselling geared towards the needs of individuals is one of the most important but generally under-valued professional activities, and students should make full use of it wherever possible.

Careers advice should take place early in the learner's schooling – preferably before subject choices are made in secondary school, and certainly before making applications to college or university.

The workplace

It is important that young people do not equate study or exam success with workplace success. There is much more to success at work than being able to learn and study effectively.

How to help – fitting into a workplace

A key prerequisite for success in any workplace is 'fitting in'. Some suggestions for achieving this are shown below. A useful website highlighting the skills that employees need is: https://www.youthcentral.vic.gov.au/jobs-and-careers/plan-yourcareer/8-job-skills-you-should-have.

☞ **Teamwork** – employers value this, and it is good practice to get to know colleagues and make an effort to interact with them effectively even during times when you are busy. Most workplaces are built on teams, and it is important to value other people's strengths and their individual contribution.

☞ **Interpersonal skills** – these are as important as study skills. Students can isolate themselves a great deal; much of studying is carried out individually. It is therefore often the case that young people have to learn to work with people of all ages and at all levels.

☞ **Communication skills** – these are essential for working effectively in the workplace. It may be easy to slip into student vernacular, but what is acceptable at college may not be acceptable in the workplace! Employers often run courses in communication with clients and in team-building. It is important that young people take these seriously, and treat them with the importance they deserve.

☞ **Planning, organising and time management** – a study skills programme should be able to help with this, but it is important to make a real effort to ensure you arrive on time and are seen as being reliable by employers in terms of organising your day and overall workload. Invariably, the job will involve dealing with different priorities and work demands simultaneously. This can be stressful, so the message here is simple – ask for help when you need it! Most people in your workplace will have encountered this, and may well have useful advice.

Experience is crucial and young people starting off in the job may not have the experience that others have; it is important to acknowledge this and ask for assistance.

- **Problem-solving and decision-making** – this is important, and it has implications for education. It is important that young people gain experience at making decisions, and this should start as young as possible. Additionally, problem-solving activities can be a fun way of learning, and can increase motivation.

- **Knowledge of technology** – this is now crucial, and should be encouraged from an early age. It is heartening that most schools now embrace technology, and most young people are increasingly adept at using apps and computer software.

- **Self-esteem** – it is important not to feel intimidated in the workplace, or to have an exaggerated sense of awe of colleagues. For that reason, work experience while still at school is important, as well as informal visits by employers and some of the staff. School needs to prepare young people for any challenges that might occur in the workplace, particularly in relation to self-esteem and confidence.

- **Listening skills** – these are fundamental to acting on instructions and learning on the job. It is important that young people know the questions to ask and are not apprehensive about asking them. They need to realise that asking questions does not portray ignorance but rather interest.

- **Adapting to the workplace culture** – young people will usually have been in an educational setting for more than fifteen years; this is a long time, and it is natural that the school culture becomes part and parcel of their make-up. But they will soon realise that the workplace culture is quite different, and they need to adapt to this. It is best to abide closely to the rules, ensure reliability and punctuality, and show an interest in the company you work for. You can try to understand how the organisation is managed, and how are decisions made. This will help you feel part of the company, and be proud of what you do.

The following website highlights the skills that employees need:
https://www.youthcentral.vic.gov.au/jobs-and-careers/plan-your-career/8-job-skills-you-should-have

Reflective learning in the workplace

Reflective learning is now an important theme in the school curriculum. It also has implications beyond school. Employers want staff to be able to reflect on their job, and devise ways of developing their work with increased efficiency. Practice at doing this at school is vital, because it provides the learner with a reflective learning mindset. Reflective learning is the conscious process of reflecting and learning from the task and the role of the worker. The key points would involve:

- Learning from a range of different situations – learning from experience is important for reflective learning.
- Being able to justify what you are doing, and the method you are using to achieve the task.
- Being able to transfer your learning to other similar situations. This shows initiative, and this is what employers are looking for.
- Becoming a confident but considerate learner. You need to be confident in what you are doing – but remember that it does not matter how experienced or skilled you are, there is always more to learn.
- Self-appraisal – you should be able to examine yourself critically and see yourself as an employer might see you. This means you need to be able to identify your own strengths and weaknesses, including areas for improvement.

Part 6: Conclusion

Chapter 28: Summary

This chapter recaps on the many factors that affect learning studying for learners – of all ages. We have indicated why these factors are important for effective learning. It is important to note that not all learners will respond to learning in the same way, and it is crucial to try to personalise specific strategies for each individual learner.

> **Key Point**
>
> Not all learners will respond to learning in the same way, and it is crucial to try to personalise specific strategies for each individual learner.

The learning climate and school ethos

The school learning climate and the school ethos have much to offer in helping students to become effective learners. Effective learning is not only an individual responsibility. It is a whole-school responsibility. It should be integral to the school system. Attention should be paid to subject content, to ensure that it is accessible. Subject delivery is also important, so that the presentation of the curriculum acknowledges the learning style of students, and planning takes into account the potential difficulties they may experience with the subject as well as their strengths, to help to extend their understanding. It is important that opportunities for collaboration with other subject teachers are provided. This can promote cross-curricular transfer of knowledge, and any particular concepts that can apply across different subject areas can be noted.

The school ethos can promote success and motivation. It is important that staff in schools recognise this, and seek to ensure that the school has a positive learning ethos and that the school environment is learning-rich. School assemblies can be an important part of this, as can music, classroom and school design, the notion of emotional literacy and opportunities for success to be celebrated at a whole-school level.

Learning is holistic

It is important to consider the emotional and social needs of students. Environmental factors are important, and these should be considered in any learning programme that is developed for students.

Positive self-esteem is crucial

This book has reiterated this point a number of times, and we cannot overestimate the importance of positive self-esteem for successful learning. This is also important for exams, because learners are more likely to take a chance and make appropriate comments on a tricky exam question if they feel they know that area and have a positive outlook. If they feel good – they do good!

> **Key Point**
>
> *There are many successful strategies that can be used by learners, and it is important that they have the opportunity to try these out and decide what is best for them.*

The importance of values

It is important that everyone is valued – students of all abilities, and all teachers and instructors. Time and effort should be made to 'stress-proof' the school. This is more than promoting individual means of reducing stress; it also means looking at and addressing institutionalised stress. It is important to recognise this as a factor that can affect student performance. Effective learning stems from an effective school.

Intrinsic motivation

Learners need to decide their own motives for tackling a learning exercise. Encouraging this is a whole-school responsibility and needs to be management-led. The learning environment and the learning experience must be motivating for the learners, and this can be achieved through the recognition of shared goals and acknowledging learning preferences. It is important to encourage self-evaluation through self-questioning, self-monitoring and self-assessment.

Consider the learning environment

This includes the design of the classroom, the wall displays, lighting and seating arrangements. Music and movement should also be considered – for many students, a silent, static environment is not the most effective one for learning.

Students need to own their learning

Ideally, the student should not be learning for exams or to satisfy the teacher or the requirements of the school curriculum, but for themselves. They need to take ownership of this. Once they assume this responsibility, it is easier to move from extrinsic to intrinsic motivation. That is what we want to achieve, because through this, students will reflect on how they are learning and make attempts to make their learning more efficient and successful.

Empowerment

It is important to empower learners to have control over their own learning. This is one of the key aspects; effective learning is about having control over your learning experience. This means the learner will know which resources to use, the length of time that can be spent on any one activity and the learning sequence, and essentially be able to direct, monitor and assess his or her progress.

Responsibility

It is important that students can take responsibility for their own learning. This means that they need to ask questions of themselves as they are learning. They need to know the questions to ask such as: "What have I to do here?", "How does this relate to what I already know?", "What else do I need to find out?" These types of question provide scope for self-reflection, and provide evidence that the student is beginning to take responsibility for their own learning.

Acknowledge learning preferences

Knowledge of learning preference is particularly useful when tackling new and challenging information. It is often best to get learners to understand their learning preference to begin with in order to obtain a better comprehension of the area of study. It should be noted that the term 'learning preference' implies a more comprehensive meaning than 'learning style' and 'preference' would also include the learning environment and the interaction between the learner and the learning materials.

The task should be set appropriately for the student – the success of learning can depend on it. It is important to ensure that the task can be successfully carried out. This means that preparation for the task is important, and steps need to be taken to ensure it is effectively differentiated for the student. This includes how the task is presented, as well as the learning outcome. Students often fail because the task is beyond them. If this is the case, then the onus is on the teacher to differentiate the task, and to break the task down into smaller steps so that the learner can succeed. However, it is crucial that learners can attribute their success to their own efforts and not to the support from the teacher. If they attribute success as solely the result of receiving support, they will find it difficult to become independent and autonomous learners.

Understanding

One of the key issues for learning and studying is *understanding*. This needs to be considered at all stages of learning, and particularly at the outset. It is too late for this when the student is at the stage of revising for exams. Understanding needs to be integral to the teaching and learning process, and it is worthwhile taking time to ensure understanding before moving on to the next topic.

> **Key Point**
>
> *It is crucial that learners can attribute their success to their own efforts and not to the support from the teacher.*

Learning is a process

It is important to consider this because it implies that learning will take place in a series of steps, and importantly these steps have to be explicitly presented. It is a good idea if the learner can see the steps being taken. They can be noted in a diagram or progress chart.

Learning takes place over time

This implies that students will need sufficient time to complete tasks, and some students may need more than others in the class. This is also important for consolidation of new learning (see point below). It is also good if reviews and recaps are built into the new learning.

Learning is more effective when the content is familiar

One of the most effective means of achieving this is through pre-task discussion. This will ensure the learners have a good grasp of the concepts and a background understanding. Students will need to engage in pre-task discussion before they can embark on a task independently.

Feedback

Feedback is important for developing learning skills. Time should be allocated to provide feedback, not only on the outcome of the task, but also on the learning process the student has gone through. It is important to enter into a dialogue with students, to discuss how they achieved and responded to tasks. This helps the students to develop self-knowledge about how they learn. It also allows the teacher to obtain a view of the student's preferred method of processing information.

Learning requires a period of consolidation

This is important for students because it implies that overlearning is necessary. Often, students may appear to have learned something new but they may not have consolidated that new piece of learning. This means that they require a period of overlearning in order to ensure they have automaticity in the use of that new learning. As a result, learning will take longer for some students, because they need longer to acquire automaticity. This should not happen by accident; it needs to be planned, and it is important to present the materials that have to be learned in different teaching contexts and also to present them over period of time. This enhances the opportunities for retention and understanding.

Prepare for learning and for exams

This is also important. Students often feel they have prepared for exams, but often all they have done is read over their notes – that is, in fact, a reading exercise and not a learning one. The best preparation for exams is to be able to ask oneself questions about the content. This has been covered in this book, but self-questioning is very important, and it can also provide a degree of confidence as it is likely the questions that the students ask themselves will be similar to those in the exam. Preparation, however, starts at the beginning of the learning process, and not just during the revision period. As soon as a new topic is introduced, the learner needs to ask him- or herself questions.

The brain is a well-oiled machine

The brain can be compared to a machine, and like all machines it needs to be cared for and looked after. The brain appears to have limitless capacity, but you need confidence that your brain can do it! Looking after your brain is the same as looking after your body. Nutrition, sleep, rest and recreation can all be as important as slogging over books for hours on end. If you have to 'burn the midnight oil', you have miscalculated somewhere! The next point refers to this.

> **Key Point**
>
> Looking after your brain is the same as looking after your body. Nutrition, sleep, rest and recreation can all be as important as slogging over books for hours on end.

Organisation is key to effective learning

This says it all – most of us now have increasing demands on our time. The phrase 'too many things to do and not enough hours in the day' has been around for a long time, but it certainly has a great deal of relevance to today's society. Children and students of all ages have great demands placed on them, and with places at colleges and universities being increasingly competitive, these demands can translate to anxiety and stress. It is important that every learner takes time to learn about organisation. Organisation is personal, but all learners should have self-knowledge and self-awareness to help them organise their time. Imposed organisation may not work for everyone, so organisation needs to be discussed and negotiated with the learner.

Organisation is the key to effective memory, and it means being able to organise and make information meaningful at the point of learning. Therefore, when making notes, the student should be able to use appropriate and meaningful headings and sub-headings, and recognise how the information can be applied to their practice, or their existing schema. They should be generating conceptual understanding at the point of learning. Often, students are preoccupied with obtaining the facts and then later try to make sense of these facts. This is too late, as much of the thinking surrounding the initial learning is lost. Students need to obtain the ideas and concepts at the point of learning, and later reflect on these from a position of understanding.

Use technology as much as possible

This can be increasingly helpful, with a large number of websites and apps available that help with learning. Some of these are shown in Appendix 1. It is a good idea if learners familiarise themselves with some of the apps, and it is important to be selective. Popular apps include 'Inspiration' (www.inspiration-at.com/resources), a powerful visual thinking tool for creating mind maps, concepts diagrams, graphic organisers, outlines and presentations. The developers indicate that this app can help students who have difficulties with short-term memory and processing information, those who can be distracted when there is too much text to deal with or have difficulties expressing ideas in writing, and those who have difficulties with the structure and layout of essays.

Chapter 29: A last word to parents and carers

In our experience, one of the key things that parents and carers want to know is how their child should study. It is vitally important to realise that learning is not a 'one size fits all' situation, so there is no single answer to how best a child should study. Instead, it's important to spend

Key Point

Learning is not a 'one size fits all' situation, so there is no single answer to how best a child should study.

time with the child, to find out about his or her way of learning. If the child is going to be able to do this, then he or she will of course have to have some insight and self-knowledge, so the process can be a bit circular at the start. The key thing here is to have these conversations with your child, to listen, and to allow him or her to explore different ways of doing things in order to find out what works best.

This approach should also help to develop the child's confidence, and we have shown how important confidence and self-esteem are for learning. Similarly, when the child's views are properly discussed and considered, there is a positive effect on stress levels. The child will feel more in control, less anxious, and in a better mindset to absorb information and work creatively with what he or she learns.

When we really engage with a child about how he or she learns, it becomes clear that some factors are internal to the child (for instance, a preference for reading, or listening, or 'hands-on' learning), but that there are many important factors that relate to the environment. Where possible, changes should be made that will enable the child to focus, concentrate and produce his or her best work.

It is also important that the child is given advice and guidance on how, generally, people learn (metacognitive awareness). Specifically, we need to link information to what we already know if we are to understand and remember it, and there are techniques that can be used to make this process easier. These techniques should be applied at the time of gathering information, note-taking and revising. There are a number of ways of helping children to revise and recall information and it is very important that they are given guidance in these areas. They will also benefit from help in planning and organising their study time (always remembering to give enough attention to relaxation), and in writing essays and sitting exams.

Finally, while guidance and support of different kinds will be necessary at different stages in a child's education, it is crucial that he or she becomes self-sufficient and ultimately an independent learner. When faced with difficulties at a later stage, the child should be able to draw on the lessons that were provided earlier, and use these to provide him- or herself with the necessary support and conditions. If this isn't possible, the child should at least know what to ask for, in order to advocate for him- or herself. This becomes very important in later studies. In helping children and young people to study and learn more effectively, parents and carers are building a foundation for lifelong learning.

Chapter 30: A last word to teachers and schools

The best thing about being a teacher is having the opportunity to see pupils flourish, grow and find success. It can be frustrating for everyone concerned when there are obstacles to this – barriers to learning that prevent some pupils from demonstrating their potential. If all pupils are to be given the chance to show what they can do,

Key Point

Pupils should be encouraged to take responsibility for their learning, and to work with their teachers to become autonomous learners.

there has to be some degree of flexibility in the learning environment, in ways of teaching, in the range of resources available to teach, and in the time that is allocated to teaching study skills as distinct from subject-specific curriculum content.

Teachers themselves must be supported from the highest level of school management, and this cannot be stressed enough. They need to have training, time and opportunity to develop and adapt their teaching methods and materials. They will also need support in helping the wider needs of pupils who are experiencing stress or anxiety. They will need time to find out about the different learning styles of their pupils, and they will need to be in a position to accommodate to at least some of their different needs.

This can seem overwhelming, when it is in addition to teaching curricular content, and particularly when exams are looming. However, an inclusive and accommodating approach really has to be seen as part and parcel of topic teaching. There is little point in getting through every item in the curriculum if a good proportion of the class has been unable to absorb or remember it.

It can be useful for teachers to work together to share information, resources and ideas, and to support each other. Some will find it easier than others to adapt their ways of teaching, and they could share examples of good practice. There should be a mentoring policy for new staff, and senior management should support and encourage an atmosphere of collegiate learning. Non-judgemental support should be available for staff who need it. Success should be celebrated.

Pupils, for their part, should be encouraged to take responsibility for their learning, and to work with their teachers to become autonomous learners. They need to be made aware that they have an important role to play in their learning, and that a passive approach will be limiting. When they take an active role, they will take in more, understand information better, and remember it more easily.

Index of *How to Help* advice

Self-efficacy and self-esteem	26
Motivation	34
Learning preferences	38
Relaxation	40
Barriers to learning	47
Embedding a positive school ethos	51
Positive feedback	53
Understanding how you learn	60
Classroom design	66
Differentiation	71
Multiple intelligences	77
Time management and organisation	84
Information gathering	88
Scanning text	91
Structuring notes	95
Note-taking	98
Using schemas and existing knowledge	104
Scaffolding techniques	106
Problem-solving skills	110
Understanding what is being taught	114
Encouraging comprehension	117
Visual learning activity	119
'North, South, East, West'	122
Creating self-aware readers	123
Making social sciences learner-friendly	125
Challenges and strategies in music and art	127
Identifying memory problems	133
Organising information	143
Creating a mind map	145
Extending vocabulary	150
Understanding essay questions	151
Essay writing checklist	153
'The Five Rs' of effective revision	157
Creating a revision plan	159
Exam stress management	166

Index of How to Help advice

Anxiety prevention checklist 168
Exam question keywords 171
Common types of exam question 174
Reflection skills 176
Top five after-exam activities 177
Writing frames..181
Taking notes from books 183
Fitting into a workplace 185

Appendices

Appendix 1: Further reading and other sources of Information

Chapter 5: Self-efficacy and self-esteem
https://youngminds.org.uk/find-help/for-parents/parents-guide-to-support-a-z/parents-guide-to-support-self-esteem/

https://www.understood.org/en/friends-feelings/empowering-your-child/self-esteem/7-ways-to-boost-your-childs-self-esteem

Chapter 6: Motivation
Reid G (2007) *Motivating Learners In The Classroom: Ideas And Strategies*. London: Sage Publications. www.drgavinreid.com

It is important to ensure that a gifted programme is available. Some useful websites are:

https://www.education.udel.edu/wp-content/uploads/2013/01/GiftedStudents.pdf

http://www.gifteddevelopment.com

https://www.youtube.com/watch?v = tiGmMfl6ndE

https://www.nagc.org/resources-publications/gifted-education-practices

https://www.weareteachers.com/teaching-gifted-students/

Chapter 7: Stress and anxiety
The following is designed to raise awareness of mental health issues using a range of mental health and wellbeing assessment instruments. *Measuring And Monitoring Children And Young People's Mental Wellbeing: A Toolkit For Schools And Colleges*. Available at: http://www.annafreud.org/media/4612/mwb-toolki-final-draft-4.pdf

Information and practical advice on anxiety for children and young people, parents and professionals. *20 Classroom Interventions For Children With Anxiety Disorders*. Available at: http://www.healthcentral.com/anxiety/school-258065-5.html
www.youngminds.org.uk

Chapter 8: Barriers to learning
https://inservice.ascd.org/10-strategies-and-practices-that-can-help-all-students-overcome-barriers/

Chapter 9: The school ethos
There has been an increasing amount of literature on positive learning (for example, see https://sites.google.com/site/tourozperrin/positive-learning).

Chapter 10: Feedback
https://www.edutopia.org/blog/tips-providing-students-meaningful-feedback-marianne-stenger

https://www.opencolleges.edu.au/informed/features/giving-student-feedback/

Chapter 11: Metacognition
Engaging and accessible guide shows students how to tailor their learning to their individual needs. Cottrell S (2019) *The Study Skills Handbook 5th Edition* Macmillan Education. London: Red Globe Press.

Chapter 12: Classroom design
Colour therapy:
https://www.youtube.com/watch?v = Dbl0Duyfpps).
www.colour-therapy.co.nz

Chapter 13: Differentiation
This teacher's toolkit contains ideas and game activities for teaching and learning.
www.crownhouse.co.uk

This book focuses on the theory of multiple intelligences proposed by Harvard psychologist Dr. Howard Gardner.
Lazear D (2004) *Outsmart Yourself! 16 Proven Strategies For Becoming Smarter Than You Think You Are.* New Dimensions Press. www.davidlazear.com

Chapter 14: Time management and organisation
Time Management:
https://www.purdueglobal.edu/blog/student-life/time-management-busy-college-students/

https://www.lib.uoguelph.ca/sites/default/files/time_mgmt_intro.pdf
https://www.lib.uoguelph.ca/sites/default/files/finding_best_time_of_day.pdf
http://www.concordia.ca/content/dam/concordia/offices/cdev/docs/time-management/finding_time_study_grid.pdf
20 Tips For Managing Your Time Well: https://students.dartmouth.edu/academic-skills/learning-resources/time-management-tips
Making a written list (called a 'task-list' or 'to-do list') of everything that needs to get done is a simple, yet amazingly powerful, strategy: https://www.lib.uoguelph.ca/sites/default/files/making_task_list.pdf

Chapter 15: Information-gathering

http://www.kathleenamorris.com/2018/02/23/research-filter/
http://www.kathleenamorris.com/2019/02/26/research-lessons/
Alistair Smith's books on learning: www.alite.co.uk
Mandy Appleyard, an educational consultant, can be found at Fun Track Learning Centre, Perth, Western Australia: www.funtrack.com.au

Chapter 16: Note-taking

Note-taking strategies:
sas.calpoly.edu/asc/ssl/notetakingtips.html
www.coun.uvic.ca/learning/note-taking/
Improving note-taking with mind maps:
www.mindtools.com/mindmaps.html

Chapter 17: Linking new information to prior knowledge

https://canvas.vt.edu/courses/62492/pages/schema-theory-in-the-classroom?module_item_id=349239

Chapter 18: Problem-solving skills

Cottrell S (2017) *Critical Thinking Skills (3rd Edition)*. London: Macmillan Education.

Came F, Cooke G & Brough M (2002) *Learning Toolkit Vol 1 And Volume 2*. Marlborough, UK: Learning Works International.
www.learning-works.org.uk

Chapter 19: Understanding what is being taught
http://www.specialconnections.ku.edu/?q = instruction/reading_comprehension/teacher_tools/teaching_after_reading_self_questioning_strategies
https://www.readinghorisons.com/reading-strategies/teaching/comprehension/building-reading-comprehension-through-questioning-techniques

Chapter 21: Supporting and improving memory
Organising and integrating information - examples and practice:
http://www.thinkbuzan.com/intl/?utm_nooverride = 1&gclid = CLD09tnH hK0CFQduhwodhFp7Lw
Introduction: www.coun.uvic.ca/learning/note-taking/organising-information.html
Concept mapping: www.coun.uvic.ca/learning/critical-thinking/concept-mapping.html
Practice in mapping: www.coun.uvic.ca/learning/note-taking/class1.html
Sequential diagram: www.coun.uvic.ca/learning/note-taking/class3.html
Hierarchical outline www.coun.uvic.ca/learning/note-taking/class4.html
Tables: www.coun.uvic.ca/learning/note-taking/class5.html

Crossbow Education specialise in games for children in reading, spelling and memory and produce game activities on literacy and numeracy.
Address: 41 Sawpit Lane, Brocton, Stafford ST17 0TE
Tel: 01785 660902
Website: www.crossboweducation.com

Memory and remembering
www.coun.uvic.ca/learning/memory/

Mnemonics memory aids
www.mindtools.com/memory.html

Chapter 23: Planning and writing a good essay
https://thewritepractice.com/writing-an-essay/
https://grammar.yourdictionary.com/writing/how-to-write-an-essay.html

Chapter 24: Effective revision
General strategies for taking tests
www.coun.uvic.ca/learning/exams/

Techniques for problem-solving and Maths and Science tests

http://mathcs.slu.edu/undergrad-math/success-in-mathematics/?searchterm = Techniques%20for%20problem%20solving%20and%20math%20and%20science%20tests#section-5

How to respond to essay questions and strategies for multiple choice exams:
www.coun.uvic.ca/learning/exams/essay-questions.html
www.coun.uvic.ca/learning/exams/multiple-choice.html

How to study: https://howtostudy.org

Study skills for students: https://www.educationcorner.com/study-skills.html
Study skills checklist: https://www.educationcorner.com/study-skills-checklist.html
How to study: https://www.how-to-study.com

Twelve apps for study skills: https://www.commonsense.org/education/articles/12-apps-and-websites-for-sharpening-study-skills

http://faculty.bucks.edu/specpop/Actfrm.htm

http://www.openuniversity.edu/resources/study-skills

Chapter 27: Lifelong learning

https://alwayslearningweb.wordpress.com/2018/12/31/7/

https://studyandcareers.ie

Appendix 2: Interactive Observational Style Index (IOSI)

(adapted from Given & Reid, 2005)[15]

Emotional

Motivation:

- What topics, tasks and activities interest the pupil?
- What topics does the child speak about with confidence?
- What kinds of prompting and cueing are necessary to increase motivation?
- What type of incentives motivate the child: leadership opportunities, working with others, gold star, free time, physical activity?
- Does the pupil seem to work because of interest in learning or to please other (e.g. parents, teachers, friends)?

Persistence:

- Does the pupil stick with a task until completion without breaks?
- Are frequent breaks necessary when working on difficult tasks?
- What is the quality of the pupil's work with and without breaks?

Responsibility:

- To what extent does the pupil take responsibility for his or her own learning?
- Does the pupil attribute his or her successes and failures to self, or others?
- Does the pupil grasp the relationship between effort expended and results achieved?
- Does the pupil conform to classroom routines, or consistently respond with nonconformity?

Structure:

- Are the pupil's personal effects (desk, clothing, materials) well-organised, or cluttered?
- How does the pupil respond to someone imposing organisational structure on him or her?

- When provided specific, detailed guidelines for task completion, does the child faithfully follow them, or work around them?

Social interaction:

- Is there a noticeable difference between the pupil's positive spirit and interactions when working alone, one-to-one, in a small group, or with the whole class?
- When is the pupil's best work accomplished – when working alone, with one other, or in a small group?
- Does the pupil ask for approval or to have work checked frequently?

Communication:

- Is the pupil's language spontaneous or is prompting needed?
- Does the pupil like to tell stories with considerable detail?
- Does the pupil give the main events and gloss over details?
- Does the pupil listen to others when they talk or is he or she constantly interrupting?

Cognitive modality preference:

- What type of instructions (written, oral or visual) does the pupil most easily understand?
- Does the pupil respond more quickly and easily to questions about stories he or she has heard or read?
- Does the pupil's oral communication include appropriate variations in pitch, intonation, and volume?
- In his or her spare time, does the pupil draw, build things, write, play sports, listen to music?
- When working on the computer for pleasure, does the pupil play games, search for information, or practice academic skill development?
- Does the pupil take notes, write a word to recall how it is spelled, or draw maps when giving directions?
- Given an array of options and asked to demonstrate his or her knowledge of a topic by drawing, writing, giving an oral report, or demonstrating/acting, what would he or she choose?
- Under what specific types of learning (reading, maths, sports, etc) is tension evident? This could include nail biting, misbehaviour, distressed facial expressions, limited eye contact.

Sequential or simultaneous learning:

- Does the pupil begin with step one and proceed in an orderly fashion, or have difficulty following sequential information?
- Does the pupil jump from one task to another and back again, or stay focused on one topic?
- Is there a logical sequence to the pupil's explanations, or do his or her thoughts 'bounce around' from one idea to another?
- When telling a story (for example, about a film) does the pupil begin at the beginning and give a blow-by-blow sequence of events, or does he or she skip around, share the highlights, or speak mostly about how movie felt?
- When asked to write a report, does the pupil seek detailed directions, or want only the topic title?
- What type of tasks are likely to be tackled with confidence?

Impulsive versus reflective:

- Are the pupil's responses usually rapid and spontaneous, or delayed and reflective?
- Does the pupil return to a topic or behaviour long after others have ceased talking about it?
- Does the pupil seem to consider past events before taking action?

Physical mobility:

- Does the pupil move around the class frequently or fidget when seated?
- Does the pupil like to stand or walk while learning something new?
- Does the pupil slump or sit up when working?
- Does the pupil jiggle his or her foot a lot?
- Do the pupil become entangled in his or her chair when working quietly?

Food intake:

- Does the pupil snack, chew on a pencil or bite on a finger when studying?
- Does the pupil seek water frequently when studying?
- Does the pupil chew on her hair, collar or button while working?

Time of day:

- During which time of day is the child most alert?
- Is there a noticeable differ:rence between morning work completed versus afternoon work?

Environment: Sound

- Under what conditions (sound or quiet) is the pupil relaxed but alert when learning?
- Does the pupil seek out places to work that are particularly quiet?

Environment: Light

- Does the pupil squint in 'normal' lighting?
- Is there a tendency for the pupil to put his or her head down in brightly lit classrooms?
- Does the pupil like to work in dimly lit areas or say that the light is too bright?

Environment: Temperature

- Does the pupil leave on his or her coat on when others seem warm?
- Does the pupil appear comfortable in a cooler room?

Environment: Furniture design

- When given a choice, does the pupil sit on the floor, lie down, or sit in a straight chair to read?
- When given free time, does the pupil choose an activity requiring a formal, or informal posture?

Metacognition:

- Is the pupil aware of his or her learning style and strengths?
- Does the pupil analyse the environment with regard to his or her learning with questions such as:
    - Is the light level right for me?
    - Am I able to focus with this level of sound?
    - Is the furniture comfortable for me?
    - Am I comfortable with the temperature?

- Does the pupil demonstrate internal assessment of self by asking questions such as:
  - Have I done this before?
  - How did I tackle it?
  - What did I find easy?
  - What was difficult?
  - Why did I find it easy or difficult?
  - What did I learn?
  - What do I have to do to accomplish this task?
  - How should I tackle it?
  - Should I tackle it the same way as before?

Prediction:

- Does the pupil make plans and work toward goals, or let things happen as they will?
- Is the child willing to take academic risks, or does he or she play it safe by responding only when called upon?
- Does the pupil demonstrate enthusiasm about gaining new knowledge and skills, or is he or she hesitant?
- Is there a relationship between the pupil's 'misbehaviour' and difficult tasks?

Feedback:

- How does the pupil respond to different types of feedback – for example, non-verbal (smile), check mark, oral praise, a detailed explanation, a pat on the shoulder, comparison of scores with previous scores earned, comparison of scores with classmates' performance, and so forth?
- How much external prompting is needed before the pupil can access previous knowledge?

References

Alloway TP (2019) *How Can I Remember All That?: Simple Stuff to Improve Your Working Memory*. London: Jessica Kingsley Publishers.

Bandura A (1977) *Social Learning Theory*. Englewood Cliffs, NJ: Prentice Hall.

Burden B (2002) *A Cognitive Approach To Dyslexia: Learning Styles And Thinking Skills* in Reid G & Wearmouth J (Eds) *Dyslexia And Literacy: Theory And Practice*. Chichester: John Wiley and Sons.

Buzan T (1993) *The Mind Map Book*. London: BBC Books.

Came F, Cooke G & Brough M (2002) *Learning Toolkit Vol 1 And Volume 2*. Marlborough, UK: Learning Works International.

Carey B (2015) *How We Learn: The Surprising Truth About When, Where, And Why It Happens*. New York, NY: Random House Trade Paperbacks.

Coffield F, Moseley D, Hall E & Ecclestone K (2004) *Should We Be Using Learning Styles? What Research Has To Say To Practice*. London: Learning and Skills Research Centre.

Coffield M, Riddick B, Barmby P & O'Neill J (2008) *Dyslexia Friendly Primary Schools: What Can We Learn From Asking The Pupils?* in Reid G, Fawcett A, Manis F & Siegel L *The Sage Handbook of Dyslexia*. London: Sage.

Copple C & Bredekamp S (2009) *Developmentally Appropriate Practice In Early Childhood Programs Serving Children From Birth Through Age 8*. Washington, DC: National Association for the Education of Young Children.

Cottrell S (2017) *Critical Thinking Skills (3rd Edition)*. London: Macmillan Education International.

Cottrell S (2019) *The Study Skills Handbook 5th Edition Macmillan Education*. London: Red Globe Press.

Crombie M & McColl H (2001) *Dyslexia And The Teaching Of Modern Foreign Languages* in Peer L & Reid G (Eds) *Dyslexia And Inclusion In The Secondary School*. London: David Fulton Publishers.

Dargie R (2001) *Dyslexia And History* in Peer L & Reid G (Eds) *Dyslexia: Successful Inclusion In The Secondary School*. London: David Fulton.

Davies M (1986) *Literacy And Intonation* in Couture B (Ed) *Functional Approaches To Writing: Research Perspectives*. Norwood, NJ: Ablex.

Davies M (2020) *Reading For Meaning, Presentation At Scottish Parliament Cross-Party Group On Dyslexia, 15 Jan 2020*. Available at: https://www.parliament.scot/CrossPartyGroups/Session5CrossPartyGroup/Minutes/Dyslexia_20200115.pdf [last accessed 15 January 2021]

De Bono E (1995) *Edward de Bono's Mind Power*. London: Dorling Kindersley.

DfEE (Department for Employment and Education) and QCA (Qualifications and Curriculum Authority (1999) *The National Curriculum For England: Geography*. London: DfEE and QCA.

Dockrell J & McShane J (1992). *Children's Learning Difficulties: A Cognitive Approach*. Oxford: Blackwell.

Dunn R & Dunn KJ (1992) *Teaching Elementary Students Through Their Individual Learning Styles: Practical Approaches For Grades 3–6*. Boston: Allyn & Bacon.

Dunn RS & Dunn KJ (1993) *Teaching Secondary Students Through Their Individual Learning Styles: Practical Approaches For Grades 7–12*. Englewood, NJ: Prentice Hall.

Edelman GM (1992) *Bright Air, Brilliant Fire: On the Matter of the Mind*. New York: Basic Books.

Ellenbogen M, Payne JD & Stickgold R (2006) The role of sleep in declarative memory consolidation: passive, permissive, active or none? *Curr Opin Neurobiol* 16(6): 716-22.

Frederickson N & Cline T (2002) *Special Educational Needs, Inclusion and Diversity: A Text Book*. Buckingham, UK: Open University Press.

Ginnis P (2001) *The Teacher's Toolkit – Raise Classroom Achievement with Strategies for Every Learner*. Carmarthen, Wales: Crown House Publishing Ltd.

Given B & Reid G (2005) *Interactive Observation Learning Styles*. Edinburgh, UK: University of Edinburgh.

Given BK (2002) *Teaching To The Brain's Natural Learning Systems*. Alexandria, VA: ASCD (Association for Supervision and Curriculum Development).

Gonida EN & Cortina KS (2014) Parental involvement in homework: Relations with parent and student achievement-related motivational beliefs and achievement. *Br J Educ Psychol* 84: 376-96.

Graziano AB, Peterson M & Shaw GL (1999) Enhanced learning of proportional math through music training and spatial-temporal training. *Neurol Res* 21(2): 39-152.

Hattie J (2014) The Kids Who Knuckle Down And Get the Right Answers Do Not Always Succeed. *Weekend Australian* **July 18**.

Heider F (1958) *The Psychology Of Interpersonal Relations*. New York: Wiley.

Ji Y, Li S & Wang C et al (2016) Occupational stress in assembly line workers in electronics manufacturing service and related influencing factors. *Zhonghua Lao Dong Wei Sheng Zhi Ye Bing Za Zhi* 34: 737-41.

Lazear DG (2004) *OutSmart Yourself! 16 Proven Strategies For Becoming Smarter Than You Think You Are*. New Dimensions Press.

Lazear DG (1999) *Eight Ways Of Knowing: Teaching For Multiple Intelligences*. Arlington Heights, IL: SkyLight Training and Publishing.

Lee YS & Jonson-Reid M (2016) The role of self-efficacy in reading achievement of young children in urban schools. *Child Adolesc Social Work J* 33(1): 79-89.

Le Mare L (2014) *How Does Parent Involvement In Education Affect Children's Learning?* Available at: https://www.edcan.ca/articles/the-facts-on-education-how-does-parent-involvement-in-education-affect-childrens-learning/ [last accessed 16 January 2021]

Lucas S (2002) Personal Correspondence in Reid G (2005) *Dyslexia And Inclusion: Classroom Approaches for Assessment, Teaching and Learning*. London: NASEN/ David Fulton.

Miller J & Strachan S (2020) *Understanding The Experiences Of Autistic And Dyslexic Women In Transitioning Into Tertiary Education: Presentation At Scottish Parliament Cross-Party Group On Dyslexia, 15 Jan 2020*. Available at: http://gtcsnew.gtcs.org.uk/web/FILES/News-resources/Understanding_the_Experiences_of_Autistic_and_Dyslexic_Women_Transitioning_into_Tertiary_Education.pdf [last accessed 16 January 2021]

Morris A (2020) *How Can Students Manage Their Energy Levels During An Exam Period?* London, UK: Believe Perform. Available at: https://believeperform.com/how-can-students-manage-their-energy-levels-during-exam-period/ [last accessed January 2021]

Nicholson L & Putwain DW (2019) We Should Just Be Told To Try Our Best. *Psychologist* 32: 38-41.

Overy K, Nicolson RI, Fawcett AJ & Clarke EF (2003) Dyslexia and music: measuring musical timing skills. *Dyslexia: An International Journal of Research and Practice* 9(1): 18-36.

Palinscar AS & Brown AL (1984) Reciprocal teaching of comprehension-fostering and comprehension-monitoring activities. *Cogn Instr* 1(2): 117-75.

Pomerantz EM, Kim EM & Cheung CS (2012) *Parents' Involvement In Children's Learning* in Harris KR, Graham S, Urdan T, Graham S, Royer JM & Zeidner M (Eds) *APA Educational Psychology Handbook, Vol 2: Individual Differences And Cultural And Contextual Factors*. Washington, DC, US: American Psychological Association.

Purkey W (1978) *Inviting School Success: A Self-Concept Approach To Teaching And Learning.* Belmont, CA: Wadsworth Publishing Company.

Putwain D (2007) Researching academic stress and anxiety in students: Some methodological considerations. *Br Educ Res J* 33(2): 207-19.

Putwain DW (2008a) Examination stress and test anxiety. *Psychologist* 21(12): 1,026-29.

Putwain DW (2008b) Supporting assessment stress in key stage 4 students. *Educ Studies* 34(2): 83-95.

Reid G (2005) *Learning Styles And Inclusion.* London: Sage Publications.

Reid G (2007) *Motivating Learners In The Classroom: Ideas And Strategies.* London: Sage Publications.

Reid G & Green S (2009) *Effective Learning.* London: Continuum International Publishing Group.

Reid G, Guise N & Guise J (2018) *The Big Book Of Dyslexia: Practical Activities For Kids And Teens.* London: Jessica Kingsley Publishers.

Reilly N (2015) *Anxiety And Depression In The Classroom: A Teacher's Guide To Fostering Self-Regulation In Young Students.* London: WW Norton Publishers.

Renaldi F (2005) *The Use Of Multiple Intelligence In The Classroom.* Perth and Kinross, UK: Kinross High School.

Rotter JB (1966) Generalized expectancies for international versus external control of reinforcement. *Psychol Monog* 80(1): 1-28.

Silver D (2011) Using the 'zone' to help reach every learner. *Kappa Delta Pi Record* 47(1): 28-31.

Vygotsky LS (1962) *Thought And Language.* Cambridge, Mass: MIT Press.

Vygotsky LS (1978) *Mind In Society: The Development Of Higher Psychological Processes.* Cambridge, MA: Harvard University Press.

Weiner B (1972) Attribution theory, achievement motivation, and the educational process. *Rev Educ Res* 2(2): 203-15.

Wray D (1994) *Literacy And Awareness.* London: Hodder & Stoughton.

Wray D (2002) Metacognition And Literacy in Reid G & Wearmouth J (Eds) Dyslexia And Literacy: Theory And Practice. Chichester: John Wiley and Sons.

Zeidner M (1998) *Test Anxiety: The State Of The Art.* New York: Plenum.

Zimmerman BJ (2000) Self-efficacy: An essential motive to learn. *Contemp Educ Psychol* 25(1): 82-91.

To keep up to date with the *How to Help* series, bookmark:
www.pavpub.com/howtohelp